Thank God I... ® Am an Empowered Woman:

Awakening Your Inner Strength and Genius...

Copyright © 2013 Inspired Authors, LLC

Published by Inspired Authors, LLC
5348 Vegas Drive, Suite 1086
Las Vegas, NV 89108

http://www.thankgodi.com
http://www.thankgodibooks.com
http://www.johncastagnini.com

All rights reserved. No part of this book may be reproduced by any mechanical, photographic, or electronic process, or in the form of a phonographic recording, nor may it be stored in a retrieval system, transmitted, or otherwise be copied for public or private use without prior written permission from the publisher.

All designated trademarks, registered trademarks, and service marks are the property of their respective owners.

ISBN-13: 978-0-9815453-5-6 (softcover); 978-1-62137-354-4 (ebook)

Cover Design: Rachel Gillespie, Cassandra Lambert
Interior Design: Tammy Blodgett

Printed in the United States of America
Publisher's Cataloging-In-Publication Data
(Prepared by Inspired Authors, LLC)

Special Thanks: Lorraine Garnett, Tracy Hill, David Gulick, Tammy Blodgett, Terri Lucas, Matt Reagan, Heather Ruiz
Thank God I... ®: stories of inspiration for every situation/created by John Castagnini.

v.; cm.
ISBN: 978-0-9815453-9-4 (v. 1)
ISBN: 978-0-9815453-1-8 (v. 2)

1. Gratitude-Religious aspects. 2. Life change events-Religious aspects. 3. Adjustment (Psychology) 4. Conduct of life. I. Castagnini, John.

This work, book or publication is not intended to be, nor should it in any way be construed to be a cure, antidote, remedy, answer, or otherwise be considered to be a substitute for professional therapy, treatment, and/or counseling. Some of the contact information for the Thank God I... ® authors may change in perpetuity.

Letter from the Founder
John Castagnini

Let's face it. You're probably NOT going to read this entire book. If you're anything like me, you want to get STRAIGHT TO THE POINT. I get it. These days none of us have time to waste.

I spent the last twenty years in the personal/spiritual development field. I'm forever thankful for the thousands of lessons and incredible teachers that I have been so fortunate to have shared time with on this journey.

Over the years I watched thousands and thousands of people attempt to "get ahead". I deeply contemplated, why do so few people actually appear to get major results?

Yes, there are so many ways to measure results. And of course, we all get different results according to our individual values. However, there was a specific key to fulfillment that only "the few" had found.

But why?

Along my road I discovered a single tremendous incongruence that was being perpetuated throughout the "spiritual development" field.

In an advertisement for Rhonda Byrnes' New Book, 'The Power' – a follow up to 'The Secret' – it states, "You are not meant to suffer or struggle."

Do you suffer? Let's get REAL... Do you suffer? If you're being HONEST with yourself...You bet your ass you suffer!

WE ALL SUFFER. EVERY SINGLE ONE OF US.

Yes, some of us appear to have more challenging circumstances, but all of us suffer in different ways.

Why try to promise people that they can get rid of HALF of themselves (suffering)? Why set people up for the impossible?

Don't get me wrong, I thank God for the personal/spiritual development field. It helped save my life, gave me a profession, and provided me an opportunity to share my heart.

That is why it's SO important for me to share with you a treasured truth that is the KEY to finally understanding "the Matrix":

WAKE UP!

YOU CANNOT BE HAPPY ALL THE TIME!
YOU CANNOT BE FREE FROM SUFFERING!

YOU CANNOT BE MORE POSITIVE THAN NEGATIVE!

Trying to get rid of half of yourself is like a cat chasing his tail. Eventually, you will give up and be back reading this book. Hopefully, some of the teachers spewing this "get rid of the negative" crap are reading this book. We will all chase "happiness," but it's impossible to be happy all the time. Wisdom is asking a new set of questions so we may better understand the times when we aren't happy. Those times have just as much value in our lives as the happy times we seek.

Yes, there is an underlying "PERFECTION" that exists in every moment (even in you).

But... that "Perfection" involves an equal amount of suffering and pleasure, happiness and sorrow, support and challenge.

What you can do is learn how to balance your opposite emotions, one by one.

You can develop a more poised presence.
You can gain wisdom in being more objective and balanced in your decision-making.

You can be appreciative and fulfilled in honoring the actuality that exists beyond our realities.

You can develop more worth and in turn more wealth.

You can learn to Thank God for what is, as it is.

The stories in this book are real-life experiences of women who have triumphed in the face of tragedy. They found appreciation for something that was, in many cases, downright torturous at the time.

These are remarkable experiences of transcendence. The amount of real life "how to" presented in the stories opened my heart wider, page after page.

My advice? Flip through the book and look for the stories that speak to you. What are you "struggling with" at this moment?

Thank God I… ® is dedicated to sharing with you how human emotions work in connection to the universal principles that guide us all. Our authors share this through their unique stories.

Our mission is to provide you with accurate information that will serve you in mastering your mind and in turn, your life.

Yes, you will struggle. As you go through our books, our online community, our seminars, and The Power of Perfection® Education, we promise to share with you the world-leading information on how to develop yourself, others and humanity.

Who knows? Perhaps you will be inspired to share your "Thank God I…" story and engage in helping us to develop minds while we touch the hearts of people all over the world.

Every one of us is an expression of the divine. We all deserve to "Thank God," and we all have a unique Thank God I…® story.

The more you embrace each part of yourself (the positive and negative stories that make up who you are), the more fulfilled your life will be, and the more you become congruent with sharing the gift of what you are here to do.

In Loving Service,
John Castagnini

Table of Contents

THANK GODDESS I MET THOSE SHINY LIGHT BEINGS
By Audrye Susan Arbe 1

THANK GOD I HAD AN ACCIDENT
By Christy Powers 12

THANK GOD I... THE NIGHT I TRIED TO KILL MY DAD
By Judy van Niekerk 17

THANK GOD I GREW UP IN CHAOS
By Cori Hill 27

THANK GOD I GOT OUT OF THE MORTGAGE BUSINESS
By Dana Byers 33

THANK GOD MY HUSBAND DIED
By Denise Van Arsdale 37

THANK GOD I WAS LET GO FROM MY JOB
By Jane Falter 43

THANK GOD I MARRIED AN ALCOHOLIC
By Rita Soman, MA, CADC III 49

THANK GOD I WAS BEATEN DOWN
By Heather Vale Goss 56

THANK GOD I WAS LOST
By Ai Zhang 62

THANK GOD I GAVE CUSTODY OF MY KIDS TO MY EX-HUSBAND
By Alice Cablayan 69

THANK GOD I STOOD UP FOR MYSELF
By Denise Gladwell 76

THANK GOD I RECOGNIZED THE BLESSING IN THE CRISIS
By Dr. Marcia Becherel 82

THANK GOD I WAS ABUSED
By Adele Green 87

THANK GOD FOR ONLINE DATING
By Christine Little 92
THANK GOD I HAVE MUSCULAR DYSTROPHY
By Heather Watkins 99
THANK GOD THE PLANE CRASHED
By Nikki Vescovi 104
THANK GOD I FOUND ACCEPTANCE
By Teresa McDowell 112
THANK GOD I FOUND FAITH
By Faith Deeter 118
THANK GOD I SPENT TIME WITH MY MOTHER
By Inez Bracy 124
THANK GOD I AM A BREAST CANCER SURVIVOR AND THRIVER
By Nilla Spark 130
THANK GOD I FELT THE LOVE BOND BETWEEN A MOTHER AND HER CHILD
By Lia Enso 137
THANK GOD I HATED MYSELF
By Mary Ann Swanson 142
THANK GOD I WAS ADOPTED
By Sarah Collinge 147
THANK GOD I AM AN EMPOWERED WOMAN
By Olivia Parr-Rud 155
THANK GOD I WAS UGLY
By Tina Marie Jones 164
YOUR JOURNEY TO SELF-DISCOVERY
By Lisa Christine Christiansen 172
THANK GOD I CAN CREATE MIRACLES
By Alida Fehily 179
THANK GOD FOR MY DIVORCE
By Dr. Dena Churchill 184

THANK GOD I HAVE FAITH
By Susie Young-Tatum 190
THANK GOD I WAS DIAGNOSED WITH DIABETES
By Wanda Muir-Oliver 197
THANK GOD MY DAUGHTER COMMITTED SUICIDE
By Jenetta Barry 202
THANK GOD I...
By Sheila Gale 211
THANK GOD I AM A RESILIENT WOMAN
By Prof. Susana Ethel de Pereda 220

Thank Goddess I Met Those Shiny Light Beings
By Audrye Susan Arbe

I am sitting doubled-over with pain, bleeding from my vagina, and dressed in an over-sized T-shirt from painting the bathroom with my then-mate, as the cab rumbles over New York's Eighth Avenue from Chelsea uptown to Roosevelt Hospital. Six weeks before my baby's official due date, my spouse counting out the streets, keeping me informed of our progress.

Doing a combination of Bradley and deep yoga breathing, I pray with my whole heart, "God, let me keep this one! You took my first pregnancy. Let me keep this one. Let me have my daughter!!!!" I am doing everything I know to deal with these excruciating cramps, knowing blood is continually dripping from me.

I had had a miscarriage three years previously in my first pregnancy, at the end of my first trimester. As a born mystic intuitive-transformation catalyst, I knew I was carrying a boy. The day I miscarried, I did my best to hold that fetus in me, fighting my own body. I was then in my loft bed. Suddenly, my body began cramping up fiercely! I absolutely screamed and howled, lurching off the ladder to the floor. I then began banging into walls – literally – to keep me afoot, preventing me from falling down, as I banged my way into the bathroom.

"NO!!! NO!!! YAH!!!!" I screeched, holding my stomach, clenching my sphincter muscles, grabbing hold of my inner body to hold that pregnancy inside.

Thank God I... ® Am an Empowered Woman:

The pain was horrendous! Because I refused to lose my fetus on the floor, I catapulted my way into the bathroom. I continued shrieking as I sat on the toilet. Against my personal will, I expelled a little bloody mass, my fetus. Fortuitously, a friend was coming over. While still in the building hallway, she heard me screaming. Thanks to her, I got to the hospital with my expelled fetus, where I was pronounced complete. During all this my mate was in rehearsals. I left him shrieking voice messages, as I was barely able to talk, so he knew what was happening pretty much as it occurred.

I was so NOT EVER going to lose a child of mine again. One time was more than enough.

So as my mate and I, in a taxi, drove as fast as possible in New York City streets, racing to the hospital, I prayed with everything in me. I made deals with Source. "Let me keep this baby, and I'll xxxxx," I promised. He/She had taken my first, and by God/dess, I was keeping this one!!! I was having my daughter!!!!! Doubled over with pain in the cab seat, I prayed and did Bradley-yoga breathing, putting myself in as much of a meditative state as I could.

"Where are we?" I asked my mate. To help me maintain some semblance of calm, my mate counted out some of the streets and gave me a play-by-play as we raced uptown on Eighth Avenue from Chelsea to Roosevelt Hospital. It was just after noon in the middle of the week, a high-traffic time.

Once we get to Roosevelt, I look down at the bloody cab seat.

"I bled all over the seat," I tell my mate, as I stagger in a bent-over position, with him partially supporting me, towards the hospital.

"Don't worry. I gave him a good tip," he responds. Unable to remember which entrance to use, as I usually go by subway, we manage to get to Ob-Gyn, me being irritable with everyone.

"You have to fill out forms," a nurse tells me.

"I'm bleeding! My baby can be coming!" I shriek.

"She's usually much nicer than this," my mate placates, grabbing whatever documents she foists upon us.

We finally get ourselves to the right place, with me on the examining table, my feet in the ubiquitous stirrups. Everyone in the operating room -- so different from our planned Birthing Room – is laughing and joking around. Some of my midwives are present, so I feel more reassured. The chief of obstetrics is, thankfully, located. Then he starts examining me, a truly uncomfortable procedure.

"Placenta abruptia!" he announces.

Immediately, everyone goes into emergency mode. The midwives are at my head, telling me I have to sign waivers for an emergency C-section, so different from the natural birth we'd planned.

"Do I really need this?" I ask them. "Yes," they respond. "It's really an emergency." So I sign.

First, though, they have to "stabilize" me as I have lost too much blood to start the C-section. So I get a needle with some kind of anesthesia going into one arm, then the other. Then the doctor determines that I am ready. So I get another needle in one of my arms and am requested to start counting down from 10.

That's when it happens. I was filled with anger, determination, and uncertainty and at the same time, something truly amazing came over me. All of a sudden, I'm in this realm filled with love, brilliance, color, and peace, unlike anywhere I had ever been that I could consciously identify. This place is gorgeous! I feel it throughout my being. Wherever this is that I am is filled with love, amazing brilliant color, just breathtakingly beautiful. I realize I am looking at several Shiny Light Beings, one of whom I seem to know well from some other existence, realm, or experience, though I had temporarily forgotten its name. These are Beings filled with love.

"Where am I?" I ask them, especially the one I "know." I feel somewhat confused. How did I get here? What is "here"? They tell me something. "No," I answer. I then track my day from waking up to my most recent memory and tell them, "I am birthing my daughter." I know I am having a girl because, first of all, I had sensed that early on, and secondly, I'd had amniocentesis at 16 weeks and had it confirmed.

"Your body may be birthing a child, but you, the real you, is here," I was informed. And truly, the real me, the me-ness of me, certainly was in this amazing space, speaking with these astounding Shiny Light Beings.

Much more was said, which I would need deep hypnosis to remember. What I do remember is loving this place. In front of me, behind my friends, the Shiny Light Beings were what appeared to me as several doors. I sensed other Beings in the background.

My Shiny Light Beings gave me a choice to live or die, in an incredibly loving supportive manner.

"It would be easier for you to die rather than live and birth your daughter," they assured me. They told me many things, including that if I walked through that door, the one to the left of where I was looking, behind them, I would have ease and comfort, something I would absolutely enjoy. This was actually, for a moment, a major temptation. What was behind that "door"? What would I experience? Since a child, I've been eager to know what happens after life. In fact, as a child, I almost obsessed about what happens when we die. How can eternity go on forever? What's on the edge? What's before and after it? I have lived my life exploring this. This is big stuff to me, always has been, and still is.

Did I think I was dead now? Never, not even for a split second, did I even contemplate that I had died. I totally knew I was fully alive and was having this oh-so-interesting experience and conversation. I was fully present in the moment.

Yes, I definitely wanted to go through that door and find out what it was, what would happen after I went through, where I'd be then. I was also scared? Where would I be? I felt, sensed, and knew that if I went through, I, the physical me that I related to as me, would not come through this experience. Was I ready for that? Mmmmmm. I am a seeker, someone with acute inner senses, born a metaphysical being, without knowing the term. Definitely different from the norm. So this was, on several levels, major temptation. How do I let this opportunity go? Live in this place? That was a big YES! Be with these Shiny Light Beings? That would be GREAT!

My actual life, at age 38, had both delights and challenges up the kazoo. I was ever juggling money. I loved my mate passionately, and he was also intense about me. Yet we had some major issues, including lifestyle, belief systems, and attitude. When he was wonderful and loving to me, life sang. When he was something else – another book — life felt truly hellish, and yes, sometimes I cried plenty. I reached heavenly grace and touched bottom with him. At the time, I would rather have spent 20 minutes with him than days with any other man.

So, yes, I loved my spouse, with and without our differences, and I deeply desired him to be the father of my child. He was my mate, my Soul Mate, and I had selected him, preferred him to any other man, and had been with him for seven years. Would I give this up to go through that "door" and be with these Shiny Light Beings?

On one level, this was a tough and courageous decision. To live meant I would have to deal with all the complications in my life, including those incumbent in being my mate's mate. Life was sometimes really tough. Did I like that? Resoundingly NO! I craved ease instead.

The Guides let me know that if I chose to live and have my daughter, there were three things I had to agree to.

Three Conditions I Had to Agree To:

I would do it alone, it would be difficult, and I would have to take off my rose-colored glasses.

So, yes, I wondered about the DOOR a LOT. I was curious. Hugely concerned that if I even took a peek – and I wanted to!!! – I would not return from wherever I was. I had miscarried my previous pregnancy. This was my one time to have my daughter, who I wanted more than ANYTHING, with the man of my choice being her dad. It was as if there was a battle going on inside of me, between my past and a new promise. I laid down to rest my past, and followed the beings present with me today.

Did I have any desire to be a single mom? Oh, H---, no! Did I look forward to difficulty? Not even close. Rose-colored glasses? I would deal with it.

Having my daughter, however, came first. I had waited my whole life to be a mother, and nothing — N - O - T - H - I - N - G — was going to stop me at 38 from having this child and being her mom.

"No!" I said almost defiantly, seemingly stamping my foot. "I am having my daughter! I am going to be her mother." I was adamant. I, in all of my 5 foot, stood up to them.

After going through all this internal turmoil, which seemed to happen both instantaneously and over a somewhat extended period of time, I chose.

"You have a healthy baby girl. You have a healthy baby girl. You have a healthy baby girl.

Suddenly, everything shifted. I, the essence of me, the me I know of as me, was lying on the operating table, my mate beside me.

"Tell me you love me," I said to him.

"I love you," he said. After he said that, I felt myself truly snap back into my body. This was the first time I felt any kind of fear.

"Is she okay? Does she have all her fingers and toes? Do you know what she looks like?" I asked my mate, concerned about our daughter. There had been recent stories in the media about babies being switched. He assured me that the correct baby-name-hospital bracelet was on our child's wrist, and he reassured me that he knew exactly what our infant looked like.

To my surprise, I found out that my mate had thought that we would go to the hospital, they would "patch" me up, and we would go home. He had not realized that our daughter would be born right then. I knew the second I saw that blood come out of me when I went to pee in the bathtub as he was painting the walls by the commode, so I was unable to get to the toilet. Then blood came out. He, who was usually the calm collected one while I was the more overtly emotional one, blanched, his mahogany face turning white, while I got the phone book and looked up the hospital number. That's what got us started. I was bleeding at 12:20 pm. My baby was born at 1:14 pm.

In the recovery room on a gurney for over 12 hours, in and out of consciousness, I was given two transfusions of blood then finally moved to my room and put in a bed. My mate held our daughter before I did. The next day, doped up on medication, something totally unusual for me, Ms Healthy Vegetarian, I felt loopy and could barely enunciate. When my tiny 3 lb 12 oz daughter was first put into my arms, I filled with gratitude to finally be a mom. Then, despite all my years of preparation, including making peace with my own mom within myself, I wondered how I was going to do this. Being a good mom was one of my top life priorities.

Fast forward to two or so years later. After much gut-wrenching emotional and spiritual turmoil, for my own good and what I considered to be the good of my daughter, I left my mate, someone I had loved passionately. We had had eight years of amazing grace, growth, love, disagreement, fun, anger, blessings, and uniqueness. It was time to go, and go I did. This was a hard choice, one of the hardest I had ever made.

Then something like four and a half years later, I see him and sense there's something wrong inside his chest. I told him to have his chest checked out. Three times I said this. He ignored it. Fast forward a couple of years, and I am informed he's in the hospital. Lung cancer.

"Why didn't you tell me?" he reprimands me from his hospital bed.

"What are you talking about?" I ask.

Then he reminds me, and I remember. Suffice it to say, he had an operation, the cancer had metastasized, and he passed on. Truly, I was fully a single mom now.

Condition One of what the Guides had said happened. I would do it alone. Though I had help, babysitters and the like, as of the writing of this story, with my daughter a grown woman with children of her own, I am awaiting my new mate.

Was raising my daughter difficult? There were times I was unsure where the next piece of money was coming from.

Thank God I...® Am an Empowered Woman:

My daughter still teases me about the time I made her little self walk throughout Manhattan because I was unable to scrounge up the money for a subway token. So did Condition Two occur? You bet.

Did I take off my "rose-colored" glasses? I had never felt I was wearing any. Truly, it has always been a challenge for me to wrap myself around the concept and reality of the greed, rage, hatred, brutality, and ignorance of people and the mammoth inequities in this world. Understand, I have every emotion of our species and have done some truly foolish things.

I thank God I found the strength to listen to the Beings who guided me. They helped give to me my greatest gift, my daughter. Have I taken off my "rose-colored" glasses? Condition Three? Finally, yes. I get it that people are operating at such different frequencies, consciousnesses, heart-levels. Is this always easy for me? No. However, it gives me the freedom to live my life and be the Transformational Catalyst, Mystic Intuitive, Healer, Clairvoyant Counselor, Spiritual Therapist, Artist, Author, Woman, Mom, Grammie, Friend that I am. I will see those wonderful Shiny Light Beings at a way later chronological date, when, by my choice, I go through that door, in whatever form that door is again presented to me, provided that it is the correct time.

♥♥♥

Audrye is a born Mystic Intuitive. A transformational catalyst, healer, clairvoyant, spiritual therapist, past-life regressionist, Ro-Hun Therapist, Light Channel, award-winning artist, and TV host, mom and grammie, she authored the 700-page book, *The Mother's Manual*, A

Awakening Your Inner Strength and Genius...

Spiritual and Practical Guide to Child Rearing and Motherhood, available at TheMothersManual.com.

"Like": Facebook.com/TheMothersManual.

Connect with us at:
Audrye.org, GoddessHeartWater.com,
 1-888-75 PEACE, 1-888-757-3223,

Email: Audrye@TheMothersManual.com. Thank you and many blessings!!!

Thank God I Had an Accident
By Christy Powers

"This is my story, not my future," I told the estranged face in the mirror once again as I had many times before. However, this morning was more difficult than the other 2,189 mornings; since the event that stole my identity with its long reaching consequences that changed my life forever.

Today was the six year anniversary of the day I yearned to erase. It was the day I wished I had called in sick, had a flat tire, and decided not to go...anything except what became of my fate. It was easy to convince myself that today it was okay to feel bad, to feel sorry for myself, and just go back to bed. I pulled the covers over my head and cursed the sun. Which regardless of my wishes, insisted on rising and peering through the blinds, intruding on the chilling darkness that surrounded me.

Why this? Why now? WHY ME? I had a life that I loved as a Nurse in the Entertainment Industry, I enjoyed horseback riding, skiing, and snowboarding. I ran 5 miles a day, played point guard on a woman's basketball team, and trained 3 times a week with my personal trainer. I was fit and liked how I looked. I was often told I was a perfect double for a young Bo Derek. Up until that point, everything for me revolved around physical looks. The verse I remembered hearing as a child rang through my head, "Seek humility or prepare to endure suffering."

April 10, 2004 was the day I will never forget. While at work on a movie set, I jumped off the back of a truck lift gate and my foot became caught. This caused my right knee to wrench around violently, dislocating my knee with force that resulted in multiple grade 3 and grade 4 (Partial and Complete) Acute Tears to the Anterior Cruciate Ligament (ACL), Medial Cruciate Ligament (MCL), Medial Meniscus, Lateral Meniscus and a Fractured Tibial Plateau.

If that wasn't enough, the fall to the ground inflicted three Vertebral Compression Fractures to my Lumbar Spine, Herniated Disks and Nerve Impingement. Then the blow to my head when it struck the concrete caused a concussion. I spent 8 days in the hospital and underwent 18 procedures related to my accident. I would spend a painful year and a half in Physical Therapy learning to walk, rebuilding strength, and regaining balance. Despite the fact that I was only in my 30's, the Doctor's all agreed I would always be dependent on some sort of walking device whether it be a walker or a cane, and I would always need assistance to continue normal activities of daily living. In an instant everything changed; my world was ripped out from underneath me. I didn't know how to cope or adjust, all I knew was I was becoming more and more distraught over an accident that was completely out of my control.

The years following my accident had taken a toll on my body as well as my psyche. Initially, I couldn't walk for a period of six months. I had a full body brace and leg immobilizer; I got around with a wheelchair and after 6 months, graduated to crutches for an additional 3 months. I vacillated between bouts of attempting to heal with great enthusiasm — wheeling myself outside to my pool for self-procured Physical Therapy sessions — to moments of complete despair.

Thoughts of hopelessness began to overcome me, and I became complacent in a very unsatisfied way. Discouragement turned into anger over my perceived injustice, to the point of complete indignation. I was furious with God for letting this happen. I became convinced that somehow this accident was my punishment for not being humble enough, because I had been too superficial and "humility was being delivered to me." I felt sure there was nothing good for me in the future, that all my best days were behind me. I became resigned to my new unwanted life of pain. Recovering from the accident was hard work, the pain always won, and every day I wanted to quit. I had daily headaches and memory loss from the concussion. At times I would be driving and realize I didn't know where I was, or where I was going.

Then there was a constant searing pain that radiated from my low back into my legs like a million hot daggers stabbing me to the bone, intermittently escalating to levels that felt like I was being struck with baseball bats and my bones were shattering. Eventually I did quit, I gave up on myself. I didn't believe I could do anything anymore. After the accident I didn't feel like I had control of my own life; I lived with daily pain, which varied from moderate to excruciating. I just existed, with little to no expectations; I had a complete mindset of defeat.

The saving grace to my dilemma came in the most unusual way. If anyone would have told me a Travel Club called World Ventures would have changed my life, I would have laughed in their face. However, through this company I met three influential people that would motivate me to make some very profound changes in my life.

The first person who saw me when I felt invisible was Martin Ruof. I don't know why he spent so much of his time listening to me and mentoring me, but I was grateful to have his ear. Something very interesting started to transform for me, I became less stuck and more focused. My belief in myself began to grow because of his belief. What I took away from our conversations was: The events of your past do not reduce your potential in the future. Unfortunate things will happen to all of us but that has no bearing on what we are capable of...ever. I don't even think he is fully aware of the obstacles he helped me move through, but I know it was his conviction that made me start to believe in myself and gave me the will to try at all.

The second person I encountered was Judalon Smyth; she added to my newfound belief and encouraged me to keep pressing forward. Even though I had quit on me, she never quit on me. Through her I saw a new way of seeing things. She taught me that if a lesson can be learned in the process, then positive experiences can come out of negative circumstances.

My third mentor was the famous Marc Accetta who is a master at personal growth and development. He became the cornerstone of it all by cementing my belief. He empowered me to get out of my comfort zone and inspired me to stay on course. He challenged me to examine what I was doing and helped me to realize that what happened was exactly what I had created. He said the key to change was as basic as me working on myself, but not forgetting who I was.

One of the many lessons I learned from my accident was that tragedy can change your life in an instant and make you a victim. But the bigger tragedy is allowing yourself to remain a victim. It's moving from victim to victor where the growth and the rewards happen. Throughout your life there are going to be events that occur that will require some pretty comprehensive decision making on your part. Your choices have the potential to make a profound impact on your life. It's really up to you.

Thank God I... ® *Am an Empowered Woman:*

I don't know where I'd be without the people who challenged my perceptions of myself and encouraged me to grow beyond my comfort level, but I know they have forever shaped my life and helped me come to a place of gratitude where I can sincerely say... Thank God I had an Accident.

Thank God I... The Night I Tried to Kill My Dad

By Judy van Niekerk

I looked out the window, lifting my head and hearing the late afternoon birds singing in the park nearby and the owls starting their day as the birds were finding their respective nests for the night. The sun on its way to start a new day in another part of the world, leaving behind a kaleidoscope of colors in the sky. I could smell that grass had been cut nearby. I wondered idly how I didn't hear the lawn mower as I checked the time on the old wall clock across the room in the kitchen.

'Heck, surely not six already,' I thought as the big hand was making its way to the number 12. I turned around, looking over the tattered, cream, three-piece suite in the living room to the small TV in the corner. Just in time to see the screen change to an image of the baby Jesus in a manger with Virgin Mary and Saint Joseph looking over him. The pealing sound of the bells droning from the TV, signaling the Angelus, confirmed the clock time.

Looking back down at the cup ring stained dining table, I thought in wonderment about the hours I lose in the heaven of my art. Escaping from the drudgery of boredom, loneliness, and constant fear; I am relieved at finding this latent talent in oil painting and sketching.

As I gathered up my pencil sketches from the day, I looked in awe at what appeared to be an almost perfect replica of the portrait on the record cover of U2's Joshua Tree. The likeness was unbelievable to me. I recognized the angular jaw line of Bono, the grunginess of Edge, the placidness of

Thank God I... ® *Am an Empowered Woman:*

Adam Clayton and the youth and beauty of Larry Mullen – my heroes, my escape from reality.

I became aware of footsteps coming down the staircase. Judging from the sound, there was a skip in his step. 'It's a bit earlier,' I thought as I gathered up my bits to clear the table.

"Shall I start dinner, Dad?" I yelled out to him in the hallway. Having reached the bottom of the stairs, he was combing his jet black hair and examining himself in the mirror, finishing off with a quick comb of his neatly trimmed moustache.

Turning to look at me as I walked past to the kitchen, there was a sparkle in his dark brown eyes, not something I had seen much of recently. I had got so used to his penetrating eyes that felt like they bore into me, revealing my soul and spirit, leaving me like I had nothing, like there was nothing left in me that was mine. His eyes could make me shiver and shake uncontrollably.

"Not for me Judy, I am going out, meeting the lads in O'Donaghue's," he replied. Feeling a weird combination of relief and desperation, I stuffed my drawings and pencils into the pine dresser drawer. My mind started running wildly, a whole evening on my own again. Trying hard not to show any emotion, I strolled out to the hallway where my Dad still stood examining himself in the mirror, and said, "Who are you meeting?" "The usual crowd, Cunningham's sister and her friend are coming along before they head back to Dublin tomorrow."

I realized that for the past week Dad had been more eager to get to the pub earlier than usual and spoke a lot about

Cunningham's sister and her mate. I couldn't put words to how I was feeling about this, but something was welling up.

'OK, time for me to disappear,' I thought and making an excuse of needing to go to the loo. I ran upstairs and locked myself in the bathroom. Staring into the mirror, not seeing myself, but looking into my eyes, searching for what lay behind them. I wondered what was behind the deep blue eyes that stared back at me?

Was it the soulless, empty girl I felt? Or was there more?

I tried to reach into my body and down into my solar plexus for a 'something' that existed there. It was something that had grown over the years, and it felt as if all of me was locked up in that something. In my own mind I called it my 'something'. Did he know it was there? Did he know what it was? He knew everything about me, everything I thought – even before I thought it.

He called me.

"Judy, can you come and do something for me?" 'Shit, that didn't work,' I thought, turning from the small wall mirror, flushing the toilet, and pretending to wash my hands. I unlocked the door and went down to the hallway. "Do me a favor and cut those grey hairs out from around my ears." As I did this, which was a pretty common event, he said "Into my bed tonight, right?"

'NO, NO, NO, NO, FUCKING NO!' I thought, my palms sweating and my head feeling like it was going to explode. Struggling to breathe, I continued with as much apparent calm as I could muster up. He saw straight through that though and started to make a joke about it.

Thank God I... ® *Am an Empowered Woman:*

I realized that I was angry; no, I was fucking furious. My palms were sweating from rage not fear, humiliation, shame, or confusion, but sheer rage. The next few minutes were a blur as I finished cutting his grey hairs. I collected up the bundle of hairs, and he was off.

I threw the hairs into the bin, put away the scissors, and walked into the living room. The television still on, I remember Yasser Arafat was being interviewed, speaking of oppression. I spun around and grabbed the dark brown, hollow wooden door between the hallway and the lounge and slammed it closed with every ounce of strength I had. It slammed closed like a quiet wet fart. Frustrated with my lack of impact, I kicked it and put my foot through the door. 'FUCK, Bastard, fucking bastard,' I screeched at the very top of my voice. 'You fucking, fucking, fucking bastard, I hate you, I fucking HATE you.'

Did the neighbors hear? I don't know, and I didn't care. They certainly were neighborly and never interfered. Energy spent from that outburst, the realization of the damage I had done set in.

Panic. I examined the damage, frantically trying to find a miracle way I could put it right or go back in time a few minutes. It was countless how many times I'd felt that way over the past few years. So exhausting. Like after the shooting, the stabbing, the event in the park with the gang and so, so many more times.

But no, the hole was there, and there to stay. A big garish ugly hole in the door of the rented house we stayed in, another victim of the tragedy in yet another rented house we had occupied along the length and breadth of the country over the years.

There was no damage control possible. Unlike when he knocked my teeth in and split my lips open, and I was able to pull them right. It took every ounce of guts I had to do it, but intuitively it felt like the right thing to do. As I ran my tongue over my teeth, I was grateful I had done so, they were not straight anymore but a lot better than they would have been had I left them.

As I lay back on the sofa, wasted, I imagined what other teenagers of my age where doing at that moment. What does a teenage girl of 17 do, how does she think, what are her dreams – what does it feel like to be a normal 17 year old?

Hours went by, as my mind wandered, staring blankly at the TV screen, observing the ridiculousness of dramas and movies when you just watch the actors say their lines and act their part, and don't get into the storyline.

I decided to get to bed before he got back. Turning off the TV and lights, I walked to the top of the stairs and turned right towards my bedroom at the front of the house. Slowly, I undressed and pulled on a short, light blue, threadbare nightdress that had gathered quite a few rips and tears, the results of previous battles.

I turned off my light, got into bed, pulled the blankets up over my head, and lay there as stiff as a plank of wood, terrified, moisture building up to dampness on the sheets around my head with my quick, hot breathing. Time stood still as I lay there continuously debating should I stay or go to his bed. Terrified of my own defiance. 'What am I doing?'

'Maybe he will forget and go to bed and forget about it'.

Thank God I... ® *Am an Empowered Woman:*

I eventually saw the headlights of his car pull into the drive as they lit up my small room, the ironing board in the corner that served as my desk, displaying the pile of books I try and study from. Panicked, quick breathing, absolute terror, shivering, and nausea – 'what am I doing? This is your last chance.'

The key in the door and his footsteps up the stairs, I could hear him turn on the light in his bedroom, go to the bathroom. He said nothing. He went back into his bedroom and still nothing.

'Have I got away with it?'

As I allowed myself to take a few deep breaths, calming myself, tentatively, I relaxed.

That was short-lived. He stormed into the bedroom, fiercely pushing open the door and slamming it against my bed. He smashed on the light and in one step was by my bed. With all his force, he punched me twice in the head, then stormed out – as quick as he had come in.

Silence. Nothing said and all calm again.

My head ringing, my ear throbbing, my terror turned once again to rage. WHITE RAGE. In what felt like an out-of-body experience, I got out of my bed, ran to his bedroom, knocked him to the floor, punched him in the face, and was jumping on his chest.

Taken completely by surprise and in shock, he was slow to react – it was over, I had power, I was going to kill him. I knelt on his chest, jumping up and down, trying to crush him with everything I had in me, at the same time lashing out at his face, punching him and scratching him. I remember I wanted to gouge his eyes out – I hated them – for all the terror he had made me feel through them.

I was retaliating for all the rapes, the pregnancies, the shooting, the beatings he had inflicted on me for over 12 years. It was close to midnight, as he only ever came home after last orders were called and the pubs closed. I was screeching at the top of my voice, nothing comprehendible coming out of my mouth; there was just too much to say, too much to retaliate for, and all the words were getting jumbled – a switch had been flicked.

Then in the hazy fog of my rage, a voice penetrated my outer madness and hit my 'something,' which then reverberated around me like a ping pong ball in a gaming machine.

"Judy, you are going to kill me."

I realized, as the words settled in me somewhere, that my Dad was not defending himself and was actually allowing me to kill him. He was just letting me know that that was going to be the result of my blind rage.

I stopped, collapsed onto the floor, spent and empty.

After many minutes, I got up and went back to my bed, tears flowing uncontrollably, just tears, not the gut wrenching crying that tears like these create, just flowing tears for an age. I slept a long sleep. I woke up and knew what I was made of. I knew what was inside of me. I knew what my 'something' was – it was all of me waiting to be unleashed.

Thank God I... ® *Am an Empowered Woman:*

I knew I would never feel that fear again. I knew my father could never violently dominate me again. I knew that I had a life in front of me that I could grasp and make anything I wanted out of it – I had the power.

I was overpowered, I took back the power, and now I was powerful. My father had broken ribs and bad bruising on his chest, black eyes, and quite a few gouges in his face. He didn't go back to the pub for a while.

He was quite tender the following day, in himself and towards me. We spoke about the incident once after that. He felt that if I continued within a few minutes his ribs were going to penetrate his lungs and possibly his heart and he would have died. He said he didn't mind dying, but didn't want me to live with that.

As I reflect back on that incident today, an adult having escaped my father many years ago, I feel a profound depth of love and gratitude for that whole experience. Not only did I take back my power that night, which has remained with me through my life, I also learned so much about myself, and so did my father. It took many more experiences and a number of years before I managed to escape my father, but from that day on, I believed in myself and my strength of spirit. I had learned to love and appreciate myself, and I knew I would live a powerful life.

This experience has made me realize that in his own way, my father loved me dearly. He fathered me in a way (possibly the only way he knew how) that made me who I am today. A woman with a powerful message and purpose in life, and for that, I am so enormously grateful to my Dad for the gifts he has given me throughout the first 20 years of my life.

He passed away a few years ago. I had the great fortune of seeing him before he did and telling him, 'Thank you Dad for everything, I love you and am grateful to you.'

In the words of my mentor, Dr John Demartini, 'Love is all there is, all else is an illusion.'

Judy van Niekerk, is a Life and Business Strategist, Author and Researcher. She transforms peoples' lives around the world daily through mentoring, speaking and training as she ignites the Loves and Talents in people through her various programs. Globally she works with individuals, companies and groups across all markets including youth – guiding them to greater levels of empowerment and enrichment.

She has successfully and completely turned her less-than-ideal childhood experiences into phenomenal opportunities, which she has capitalized on to empower millions around the world to see that the challenges we experience are stepping stones for us to grow from.

She demonstrates from her personal experiences that we truly do possess the power within to create the life we love and abundance – as she says 'it is nothing more than a choice, a simple decision that will irreversibly alter your life forever.' Her other books include Against the Grain co-authored with Brian Tracy and IVF-Birthing Your Entrepreneurial Success™.

Having studied Social Justice at Strathclyde University in Glasgow, she now spends any free time studying Quantum Physics, researching all aspects of consciousness and accessing the Universal Intelligence.

Thank God I... ® *Am an Empowered Woman:*

Judy currently lives in the UK with her husband and soul mate, Tiny. They travel the world, hiking, sailing and SCUBA diving.

For more information on Judy van Niekerk, visit: www.JudyVanNiekerk.com

Thank God I Grew Up in Chaos
By Cori Hill

Lying in the soft, cool grass on a hot summer day, looking up through a ceiling of majestic trees, catching glimpses of the blue sky between swaying branches, and taking in all the fresh, clean scents of the outdoors is the best way to sort through my day and put things into perspective. Some of my favorite times have been moments like this. It is here that I think about what a wonderful life I have as an only child. I have all the privacy I want, parents who love and spoil me, who are devoted to each other, all my favorite foods upon request, along with fun shopping sprees. My daydreaming is interrupted as I realize I am five minutes late getting home, and mom is going to kill me!

Running like a crazy woman, nearly killing myself as I trip on the crack of an uneven concrete sidewalk, I am jolted back into the reality that I am the oldest of seven children. I share a room with two other sisters, most of my clothes are hand-me-downs, when it comes to food 'you get what you get and you don't throw a fit', not to mention that my parents are divorced. I've never known my real dad, and I live with a very unkind stepfather, who makes me call him dad. As I desperately try to get home, I can't help thinking about how I'm supposed to be there right now to watch my sisters and baby brother, while mom does the grocery shopping. She is the youngest of seven children herself and knows that to keep a large family running smoothly and efficiently you have to plan your work and work that plan. Every minute matters because we run on a tight schedule… and now I'm late!

Thank God I... ® *Am an Empowered Woman:*

At the time, I didn't realize how incorporating my mom's values and priorities into my own life would play such a key role in my future, but they became the core of how I do things today. Blended families are never easy and mine was no exception. Every member struggles with their own unresolved pain, unrealistic expectations, anger and resentments with little or no help to get through it, and you do the best you can. I certainly had my own issues to work through.

There were a lot of kids in our house, and with a lot of kids, come a lot of friends. If our house had a name it would be called the 'House of Chaos,' not because it was unorganized or out of control, but because it was always full of people, and everyone seemed to do their own thing simultaneously, oblivious to what was going on around them. It was not uncommon to have a talent show going on in one room, with screeching vocals that would make Alfalfa from the Little Rascals seem like a gifted singer, or an elaborate dress up, Miss America Pageant happening in another part of the house, where someone was gleefully crowned with a makeshift headband that was worn proudly by the winner as she did her fancy walk and special wave, completely ignoring the wailing contestants on the sidelines, bitter from not receiving the crown themselves.

You could hear music being played loudly from somewhere upstairs with an annoying thumping on the ceiling that comes from someone trying to finesse their dance moves, while another group of people were watching something on television that prompted loud, abrasive laughing of all sorts. Laughing that sounded like someone had the hiccups, laughing that sounded like a machine gun was being fired and I felt the need to duck every time I heard it, the pig snort laughing that is just never cute no matter how old you are, the evil witch laugh, and as things began to crash and fall, I knew someone had the silent laugh going on. You know, the kind of laugh you really never hear, but the person is rolling all over the floor, knocking things over, slapping their knees. And then, there was ME. I was just trying to study and do homework, only to be interrupted by the occasional kid wandering in from outside with a nasty, disgusting 'treasure' they couldn't wait to share.

Walking into the TV room, I turn the volume down a bit, put my finger to my mouth so my sisters know their volume needs to be turned down a bit, too, and I make my way to the beauty pageant. There, I congratulate and hug the beauty queen, while reminding her she needs to use her inside beauty to love on her friends and make them feel special. After distributing tissues to the sobbing crew, and giving a double thumbs up to the talented singers, I make it upstairs to request some quiet.

However, after being thoroughly ignored, I make my way back to my schoolwork. With a heavy sigh, my entire upper body falls onto the table, landing across my folded arms. When was it exactly that I became my parent's designated helper, the chauffeur, the playmate, the problem solver, the tutor, the storyteller, the peacemaker/referee, the 'boo-boo' nurse, and the unwilling, bad cook? I had a small window of time to get my schoolwork done. Life in my house was never boring, but it was certainly exhausting. Dropping my pencil and placing homework on pause, I find a container to hold the little shared critter and my heart is filled with love, as I see the happiness from such a small act. I yearned to love, to feel love, to be loved. I felt so insignificant.

Evenings were the worst. Once my stepfather came home, any fleeting moment of happiness vanished. Hurtful things were always said or done, arguments got out of control, with no boundaries or intervention, and most of the members of my family grew up feeling badly about themselves. I couldn't wait to leave home! I craved a better environment and often sought refuge and safety among my grandparents, church, and the family of close friends, who took me in as their own. I was determined to find a life completely opposite of what I had at home.

I found this refuge in the eyes of the children around me. I was obsessed with making sure that no child would feel that I was not there to hear them. Every child deserves to be heard. I may have felt ignored, but I could help change the world by listening to the child still locked inside of me by serving the hearts and the souls of tomorrow. It was no surprise to anyone that I got a degree in Elementary Education. There have been times when I've walked into restaurants with friends, only to randomly lock eyes with a child, who goes into Linda Blair, Exorcist mode with his head just to follow me and keep staring, then come darting straight to my table, stand by me, wave, smile, or strike up silly conversations until the parents drag him away! No one ever believes that I don't know these kids!

Similar situations like this happen wherever I go. The more experience I gained within the classroom and the more involved I became within my community, the more aware I was of kids all around me who felt misunderstood, powerless, and limited in ways of expressing their frustrations. They stumbled through their daily lives feeling defeated. There were others suffering from abuse, neglect, abandonment, stereotyped, labeled, and just unloved. The fragile, emotionally wounded children, who were still brave enough to muster up the sweetest smiles all the while their pain undetected by many, amazed me the most. I realize now that all of these kids are mirrors of me. I was this fragile, misunderstood, powerless child. My attraction to them was to help them and in turn, help heal a part of me.

The kids who have had every decision and choice made for them and very little responsibility given to them are now required in class to do these things well. There were kids who were given way more choices at home than they were capable of making. The issues went on and on. If I was going to be an effective teacher, I couldn't ignore what these kids were bringing into my classroom. It became my mission to listen to all of these kids. I did not feel listened to as a child, and I was going to give listening to them every ounce of effort.

It's impossible to work with children and not be involved with their families or interact with their parents. As my methods of teaching became very successful, parents began noticing great changes in their kids at home, too. They begged for me to share ideas and to create plans for them to use so they could get the same results at home. By partnering with parents and using local resources, I addressed the challenges and concerns they faced with their children and within their families. This process became as common as doing my weekly lesson plans and eventually launched me into a career of doing Family Assessments.

During this time, I began to realize much of my success was due to the family I had spent so much time trying to get away from and had complained about. The more I tried to change or fix them, the more miserable I became. By letting go and just accepting my family for who they are, letting them be responsible for their own choices and me for mine, huge freedom was brought to my soul. I was able to start loving them again and found a new peace in my heart.
In working with children I was able to see myself inside of them. There is nothing more valuable to me than the connection I have with these kids. I spent so much of my life feeling disconnected, as if there was something wrong with me. Wow, I could see that all of these insecurities were

pushing me to connect from my heart. Additionally, all of the challenges that I faced as a kid were pushing me out of my comfort zone. I was pushed into attaining security from the only place one can ever find it, from within.

I've learned to protect myself by setting boundaries and using my voice to stand up for what I value and care about. Each person played a significantly beautiful role in my life. By throwing myself into the service of others and working so extensively with children, my own life began to heal. Was I really the teacher or had my students been the ones teaching me all along? When I had tried to run from the pain my family had caused me, I found that, that pain just followed me in the form of other relationships.

I now believe that nothing happens to us by accident. The things we do not have the power to change are meant to mold and make us into someone very special. Facing the things that had hurt me and making a plan on how to deal with it, not avoid it, was epic! When positive things are not so apparent, I take the negatives and use them to inspire me towards a more balanced path in life. I have learned to thrive not just survive. I thank God for having so many kids in my family. I thank God for all the kids I've ever had in my classroom. I thank God for all the kids who just wander into my life. I love them all!

♥♥♥

Cori Hill lives in Houston, Texas and is the mother of two daughters, as well as a new grandmother. A longtime teacher, trainer, educator, and family consultant, Cori is passionate about empowering parents and their children. She greatly enjoys serving within her community and can often be found volunteering or at the beach. Cori would love to address your group and is available for speaking engagements throughout the year.

Thank God I Got Out of the Mortgage Business
By Dana Byers

As I hung up the phone in utter disbelief, I couldn't believe what I had just heard. My life was being threatened. My body was shaking, and my stomach was about to lose its contents. It took all I had to pick the phone back up and dial the police. My voice was shaking as I explained that a man was coming to my office with a shot gun to do bodily harm to me. I had just gotten off the phone with his wife who was in hysterics over her husband's actions. I had delivered unpleasant news to them the prior day, after weeks of trying to put together a deal for them. The police were able to pick him up a block from my office. I was so relieved to get the phone call that they had him. I was safe.

I was safe... was I really? This was a question that plagued me every day. My stomach was in constant turmoil. My health was spiraling down. My emotions were sporadic at best. My relationships were unhealthy. I was alone. I badly needed a change. I needed a change soon or the future wasn't going to exist. I couldn't figure out what went wrong. All I wanted was to help people acquire a dream. I worked hours upon hours 7 days a week to accomplish this... all in the best interest of the customer.

It wasn't enough. I knew it. I looked around at my life, and nothing made sense. I was utterly alone. I had designed it that way. I was afraid. I was afraid of people's intentions. I looked over my shoulder all of the time with anticipation that someone was out there. I landed in a foreign country about to embark on the beginning of a short sabbatical. I was meeting a very dear friend along with 2 others. Did I know what I was doing? I didn't even know the exchange rate. I booked my trip in less than 10 days.

I looked around and took in all that I could. This was such a typical pattern for me. When faced with conflict, I fled. When it came to a flight or fight response, it was definitely flight. Yet flight, in this case, wasn't the answer. I was there for three and a half weeks, and the time there resulted in illness. I went to get away and couldn't get away from myself. I took my problems with me and ended up sick. Now I was sick and alone and just as confused as ever.

Following this trip, I was still convinced that away was where I needed to be. Why face my reality when I could substitute it for something else?

I went overseas, came back and took care of my grandmother, went overseas again, and still possessed the same personal reality. I couldn't escape the feeling of restlessness and searching. I knew I had to make some kind of change but when and where? After four years plus of riding the roller coaster of indecision and escape, finally things began to take a turn for the better and the worse.

My grandmother's health took a turn for the worse, and I knew where I was needed. She was in independent living originally, but was struggling with the will to live. She was intentionally affecting her health negatively and was then placed in assisted living care. Since her mental capacity was also declining, I became her power of attorney. She was no longer able to make sound decisions. It all climaxed with her taking a fall and lying helpless for four hours. The only alternative was a nursing facility. My family was convinced that I would care for her, so I did, sometimes without the support of the rest of the family. For the next year I cared for her and watched her deteriorate. Facing her imminent death I knew my purpose was ending. I was out of town when she went into a coma, but immediately returned and was with her until her final moments.

From that experience I learned that I was indeed an empowered woman. I had run from fear in the past, but this time I stood, and I stood strong. I had the ability to face fear when it counted. I had the ability and the compassion to selflessly serve another.

When I first fled I was very disappointed with who I was. After I stood strong I realized that the pilgrimage allowed me to see that I am a free spirit who is not easily confined to a regimented business. I remember being in a spin class in a foreign country and coming back, looking in the mirror, and deciding that I was going to be OK. I had many previous mirror experiences that led to other conclusions.

Now I was actually getting to do so many of the things I had always wanted to do and coming to terms with myself. I also learned that I have a great deal to contribute to people. My grandmother, and my care for her, affirmed that. So convinced was I that I needed to be her ultimate caregiver that family members even began saying to me that I needed to prepare to move on. They could see how consumed I was with this noble purpose. This helped to define more and more the direction I wanted to go.

The tides had turned. I was now coming to see a place for stability in my life. With the passing of my grandmother, I had to move on and not back... I also needed to do something to meet my needs of purpose and productivity. I established a residence, a home base, and began a new business pursuit.

Thank God I... ® *Am an Empowered Woman:*

I am so thankful for the bad experiences that pushed me out. Even though I fled, rather than faced, some things immediately that I needed to face, the flight had its place. I was able to find out things about me that I needed to know. Things that are imperative for decision making in the future. Things that help me make choices that amplify my strengths and passions and help me balance my weaknesses. I am so thankful that something so destructive became a channel for something so healthy. I have learned to love myself in fight and in flight. I have both and both serve me to be me....

Dana was raised in a small town in Colorado. She went to college and received her Bachelor degree in Business Finance. She worked in the mortgage industry for 18 years. The last 9 years she started and operated a very successful mortgage business, after which she travelled extensively in search of her next chapter.

Thank God My Husband Died
By Denise Van Arsdale

On one particular night in February, 2001, saying goodnight was as routine as anything else in our marriage. I reached over to kiss Tom goodnight, and all I could manage was a light peck on his cheek since he was curled up and tucked under the covers. As I was turning out the light, I said half-jokingly, "I guess after 14 years of marriage the romance just isn't like it used to be." Before my head hit the pillow, Tom's response was, "No, things aren't like they used to be."

Without thinking, I sat up with my heart pounding in my ears, turned on the light, and asked him exactly what he meant by that. I watched as he tensed his face, stared deeply into my eyes, and began telling me about his six month affair with a woman he had met at work. How could I possibly get the words out of my mouth, the unbearable question of "are you in love with her?" He said that he thought he might be.

This was not the first affair he had admitted to having over the years, some of which he had while on location working in the film industry. For a few minutes I sat there dumbfounded, not believing what I had just heard while my body began shaking uncontrollably, and then the sobs just poured out from the very depths of my heart and soul.

Who was this man sitting here with me? Wasn't he the loving husband and adoring father that loved his family unconditionally? His friends knew how devoted he was, that his family meant everything to him. I would visit Tom on the movie set and everyone would be up to speed on the kid's latest milestones or any other events that took place here in the West home. He would come home from work at night and no matter how tired he was, greet everyone with a big hug and kiss and of course, that famous Tom West smile that would always melt my heart. After working 80 hour weeks with little sleep, he would help with the kids and be involved in family or school events. This was my husband who gave me greeting cards that were written better than the cards themselves. Tom was everyone's best friend. He went out of his way to help people.

What was happening to us at this very moment? For 11 years I stayed home with the children, feeling like a single mother raising them alone while Tom worked endless hours in the movie industry. I kept a nice home, cooked fabulous meals, took care of our animals, and made our life as comfortable as I knew how. I loved my husband with all my heart. My family was my world, and at this very moment, my world was crumbling to the ground. It felt as if someone had pulled the pin of a grenade and threw it at me, spewing parts of my soul out into the universe.

Tom got out of bed and began getting dressed to go to HER place, thinking this was the best course of action he should take. I begged him to stay since it was getting late, and I had to make sense of all that had just taken place. In his head he had already made a plan for himself. He moved out the next day. The kids did not know, since he usually left for work before they were up and got home when they were in bed.

After the catastrophic event that had just taken place, I did my best to go on about my days, taking care of the necessary chores and attending to the needs of my eight and ten year old children. I felt like a robot trying to deal with the horrible feelings, knowing that just a few days earlier I had actually become a single mother, possibly forever. Keeping the tears and emotions inside was an arduous task, especially around the kids, but I was able to allow them to flow freely while being comforted and supported by my loving family and friends.

At the end of the week, Tom had an appointment with his therapist to discuss how he was going to tell the kids that he was no longer living with us. He came over afterward and tried his best to tell Kyle and Alexandra that even though he loved them, he couldn't live here any longer. Kyle ran out, slamming the door, and my poor little girl began crying her heart out as she loved her daddy more than anything. With that, he got up and left.

It all makes sense to me now. In the fall of 2000, I started to feel extremely anxious and wasn't able to sleep, sometimes for days at a time. At one point, I went to the emergency room for an EKG only to determine it was anxiety and not a heart attack. I had no idea why I was feeling this way, nothing had changed in the daily routine of my life. During this time I had a couple of panic attacks, which were very scary, again not knowing what was happening to my body. On a sub-conscious level, I suppose I knew something was wrong and with the help of medication, finally got control and began sleeping much better.

During the next few months, my fears would surface around supporting the kids and myself, not knowing if I would end up homeless as my husband was enjoying his new life as a bachelor with a younger woman. Everything was out of my control, and I felt powerless. The only way I could function was tapping into my deep spirituality, knowing that God was taking care of everything. I continued to pray, asking for the help and strength to get through each day of this horrible ordeal.

Thank God I... ® *Am an Empowered Woman:*

While Tom was happy living in his new home in the Hollywood Hills, he continued to live by his word and financially took care of us. On the weekend, he made the effort to spend time with the children. I watched him change not only on an emotional level but also in his appearance. He cut off his beautiful wavy hair, shaved off his mustache and started wearing baggy jeans, like the teenage boys. I noticed that this midlife crisis was taking a toll on him — he was losing weight and aging dramatically.

Tom and the kids celebrated Mother's Day by giving me three large bouquets of beautiful flowers and other very nice gifts. For the first time in a long time, I felt special, loved by my family. Tom admitted he still loved me, but was experiencing his crisis, and reassured me that none of this was my fault. All of this wonderful attention melted my heart, but not for long. Three days later, I unexpectedly received divorce papers in the mail. Once again, I was caught off guard, and my heart was ripped apart. I suppose it was time I realize that he was serious about moving on with his life, which wouldn't include me.

August is a time of lots of celebration in the West home since my kids and I have our birthdays in the same week. For their birthday party, we decided to take the kids to an amusement park. Tom came along to share in the festivities. It was a wonderful time, riding the roller coasters together and having a real family day. Within the next few days, he admitted to missing his family, and having thoughts of a possible reconciliation. That was short-lived, as he decided he could not leave his current situation. The divorce proceedings continued in full force. I felt like I was on a roller coaster ride, and Tom was completely controlling the ride.

On November 9th, I came home from work and retrieved my voicemail messages. All I could hear was the shaky voice of a woman telling me that Tom had been admitted to a hospital in Burbank and had suffered a severe stroke. Once again, every nerve in my body began to tremble as I had to pick up my kids at school and get to the hospital. When I saw him, Tom could not speak and had no use of his left side. He barely knew I was there, would squeeze my hand, but then continued to fall back asleep. There was no communication from him otherwise.

The next day, I took the kids to see him, but since he had been heavily medicated, he was snoring like a bear. They didn't have a chance to speak to their dad. While Tom was in the hospital, and we were still married, once again I became Mrs. Tom West. What a powerful feeling that was while the nurses had to ask my permission who could and couldn't see him. For the next two days, Tom was surrounded by friends and family while we were informed of his deterioration. The stroke had affected his brain, which was slowly dying.

I was told on the fourth night that he probably would pass the following day. When we arrived at the hospital, he had already passed as the nurses had turned off the ventilator. At the age of 46, I became a widow. In a way I felt as If Tom was sacrificing himself for me and our family. I felt that Tom knew how important he was to me and that he returned the only way he knew how. Through Tom's transformation I began to see our picture so much more clearly. I realized his experience with another woman did NOT make our love any less. In letting go of my fantasies and illusions I began to learn what it meant to love myself. Tom gave to me some of the greatest experiences in my life. He also gave me my greatest challenges. I learned to appreciate both. I learned that I am more than both. I learned that no matter what I saw in Tom is in me, and that he is with me as much now as he was when we were married and splitting up. I firmly believe that God has a plan for us and everything happens in divine time. It teaches us to rise above and learn from our experiences.

My husband passed away nine years ago from a severe stroke, and I found myself in the depths of despair. After years of personal transformation, I found the courage to overcome adversity and move forward in my life.

In 2009, I became a Certified Life Coach while dedicating my life's work to helping women whose lives have been adversely impacted, assisting them in healing so they will be able to face new beginnings for living life with passion and purpose.

Thank God I Was Let Go from My Job
By Jane Falter

I kept checking the clock. The minutes seemed to drag on forever. It was the day I would learn if I got to stay employed or would be shown the door. Finally, it was time. As I walked down the hall, I wondered how I would feel when I went back to my desk.

I tried to be optimistic, but I couldn't shake the dread that filled every fiber of my being. As I sat down in the seat designated for me, I looked at my boss and the HR Rep. Their faces were frozen — all business. There was now no doubt in my mind. This would be it.

My supervisor finally began. She reminded me about how the role of the HR Partner was changing and how more and more is required of them. "Your clients said you have done a great job for them. Everyone I've talked with says how much they like you." I sat quietly, waiting for the "but". There it was… "but the demands on HR are changing, and you just aren't strategic enough. Therefore, we are terminating you. You have 2 months."

I was able to find enough voice to ask, "Isn't this something I could work on to improve? A performance improvement plan?" No. No opportunity to salvage the 10 years I had already spent there. Nothing. The decision was made. Just go. I felt rejected, humiliated, and I was so unsure. I was indeed insecure to say the least. I had so many responsibilities, and now I felt that I had nowhere to turn.

I was determined not to cry — but I didn't know how long I could keep that promise to myself. Ironically, being in human resources, I was often the HR Rep at similar meetings that transpired many times before. But despite knowing the drill, the two people sitting across from me continued to recite the prescribed script. I heard myself thinking over and over, "Don't cry, don't cry…"

They seemed to drone on forever until I was bolted to attention when I heard, "Your retirement account is included in this envelope…" I had an instant tornado of thoughts in my head. "Retire? Yes, I'm 60, but I don't feel it. Do they think I'm too old? I can't afford to retire. I have things to do. I'm not ready to stop working. I'm not ready to retire. Do they think I am too old? Is that why I am being fired?"

Finally, the meeting was over. In just 30 minutes, my whole life changed. Walking back to my office, I was keenly aware of my surroundings. Life simply went on as usual for everyone else. It didn't seem fair.

My head was spinning as I drove home that day. I had two months to figure out the rest of my life. My mind was racing — full of emotions and thoughts. Haven't I been saying I hated it there? How many times did I quip "give me a package?" Did I cause this to happen by talking about it so often?

How would I tell my daughters? Luckily, they were on their own. How do I tell them I was fired? Although I assured them I would be fine, I wasn't convinced myself.

It hadn't been a good year. My mind replayed the past. Nothing I did seemed to be enough. Having worked most of my career at small companies, I no longer had the power to make the changes I thought were right at this mega-company. Policies and initiatives were decided 'on high.'

Then they would change their minds and the cycle would start all over again. I was worn out and it showed.

Despite my unhappiness I tried to hold on just a few more years. I needed 5 more years to have enough money saved for retirement and to pay down my credit card debt. Ready or not though, it was happening now. I wasn't ready. Would I lose the house? How could I keep the mortgage up?

Although my world changed, life went on at work. My name was left off meeting notices. Some people expressed their shock and sadness. Others ignored me like a virus they might catch. I watched how they changed their path when they saw me coming so they didn't have to talk with me. Particularly hurtful were those people I thought were my friends who ignored me.

I was grateful I was given time to focus on the future. I had known what I wanted to do… but the fear of losing my secure paycheck kept me frozen. I wanted to be a life coach. The fears in my head would argue with each other like a conversation. "I know nothing about starting a business. What if I failed? What would I do without a secure paycheck? Could I ever make enough to live on? Did I have what it took to be a good coach? Should I save the money instead of spending thousands on the program?" I was petrified, yet I had no doubt this was my chance to do it. I had no doubt — I knew this "kick" was a billboard from God telling me in no uncertain terms to get the hell out of there. I oscillated between feeling helpless and alone to feeling guided towards my heart, my being my purpose. There was a glimmer of certainty hidden within the uncertainty I faced. In the real world I had responsibilities, and I was terrified at not being able to live up to them.

Thank God I... ® *Am an Empowered Woman:*

I did my research and decided on the program to get my coaching certification. I'll never forget the day I hit that "submit" button on my application. Gulp. My class started a few weeks after my position ended. That was 5 years ago...

Looking back, pushing that "submit" button was the action that opened the release valve to my heart. Being coached help empower me to believe in myself. I learned to listen to my heart and realized that it would guide my head. I soon counted on my heart to give me direction as a trusted friend. This friend was never wrong. Just because I would follow my heart though, didn't make it easy. I felt that moving south was right, but how could I move away from my friends? My fears still rose up to greet me. I still worried, but I counted on my heart to be right. And it has never let me down.

I knew I wanted to become a coach — but what kind? When I left my corporate job, I wanted to step away from anything that had to do with business or human resources. After I moved and settled into my new home, a thought kept bubbling up. I tried to ignore it, but it wouldn't go away. I knew I had to take another look.

I knew that my experience and what I'd learned in corporate America could be a great support to others who, like me, had suffered with the economic downturn and layoffs. Could I really talk about the struggles I had? Would people think I was a failure? If I could rise above my personal shame, surely I could help others get over their own suffering and move forward.

My first step in that direction was starting a career club. At first, I had no intention to make careers my coaching niche, yet that's exactly what happened. I discovered how terrible my club members' resumes were and took another step to get a certification in resume writing — just to make sure I was able to offer my clients the best!

When I walked out the door of my former company that last time, it was the beginning of a totally new journey. I have 6 completely different business cards that have marked that journey, and I am confident there will be more.

I now have a deeper wisdom and perspective of my entire career and especially, the last few years. While I had felt like a failure, there was no fail about it. Matter of fact, the reason I couldn't fit in was because of the strengths that make me who I am.

Losing my job freed me to come home to me. I recently listed all my strengths — creative, a great writer, personable, and music. I was surprised to realize that all of them were actively being used in my work. (Okay, maybe not the music so much, but playing the piano does help me relax.)

It's become crystal clear as to why that job wasn't a fit for me... Being required to implement "programs/initiatives" that didn't feel right to me and were against my inner core values, would of course, deplete my spirit. Since I realized this, my feeling of failure was replaced with pride that I had "too much going for me" to just float along.

Frankly, I don't know where my heart will lead me next. I no longer have a need to figure out where that might be. I will continue to listen and continue to follow, and when my inner guidance system says, "turn right," I'll turn right. Thank God I lost my job. It scared me to death and in the process it helped give me the strength to overcome my fears and truly live.

Thank God I... ® *Am an Empowered Woman:*

Now more than ever before, we live in a time of so much uncertainty. It may take every ounce you've got, but I am convinced that if you go deep enough, you will find the strength that will guide you. In following this guidance you will be supported and learn how to thrive as opposed to just survive.

There is a saying that God dreams a bigger dream than we can. It sure has been true for me!

Jane Falter, ACRW, SPHR, CPC, is a career coach and certified résumé writer with 30+ years' experience in human resources and a background in multiple industries including manufacturing, distribution, non-profit, and pharmaceutical. Jane has worked in mid-sized companies as well as multi-billion dollar organizations.

Thank God I Married An Alcoholic
By Rita Soman, MA, CADC III

When I was offered the opportunity to share my story in this inspiring book, I didn't know what good came out of my painful past of being married to an alcoholic man. As I began comparing where I was nearly 30 years ago to where I am today, I realized the most challenging of circumstances profoundly influenced my journey. These emotional events have allowed me to grow and create a life I would never have dreamed possible then.

Ah, love. Amazingly, it can be an exalted state where we are empowered to be our best, and just as easily, it can be the absolute worst state where we are left feeling disempowered and unrecognizable, even to ourselves. It was my fate to experience the latter many years ago.

"...But love is blind, and lovers cannot see what petty follies they themselves commit." William Shakespeare wrote these famous words over 400 years ago in The *Merchant of Venice*. Blinded by love sounds so incredibly romantic, doesn't it? I, too, was swept up by the notion of love when I met my first husband. What was not so romantic was my inability to see his harmful behaviors and the impact it would have on me. As I look back, I realize I wasn't blind to love; I was blind to the person. I chose an abusive, alcoholic and unhealthy relationship. Much would be revealed to me over the course of many trials and tribulations. Ultimately, ironically it was this abusive relationship that lead to my greatest emancipation.

I endured six excruciating years of mental, physical and verbal abuse by my snake-charming husband, the man whom I originally thought was perfect for me. Why is it the victim is the last to see the harm they have placed themselves into until the stakes have become dangerously high? I felt so ashamed that everyone knew my first husband was an alcoholic but me. How could I have stepped over this obvious behavior? Worse, my parents bitterly opposed the marriage from the start, but their protests went unheeded as I willingly marched toward the arms of my tormentor.

Our marital bliss was short lived as his behavior became more unpredictable and I became more fearful of him. He threatened to kill us both if I ever left him and so with no imaginable alternative, I surrendered to him, the alcoholism and the abuse. Every hour with him felt like a year of terror. My charismatic husband had turned into a diabolical persecutor. I felt lost and powerless. Surely, I, his loving wife, could convince him to stop this rapid descent into the abyss of alcoholic addiction, but despite my nagging, cajoling and tears, he became more abusive and controlling and I became more miserable for the life I had chosen.

As my husband's alcoholism advanced, I grew unhappier and was suffering under extraordinary mental stress. Somehow, in the back of my mind, I felt I deserved to be punished. Sadly, not only was he harming me, but I also began to harm myself by neglecting my health and smoking cigarettes. I felt trapped. There was nowhere to go. I certainly couldn't share my pain and suffering with my parents... Luckily, my younger sister and a few friends were my salvation. They listened to me, supported me and encouraged me to leave this man.

I thought I had experienced every nasty thing that could happen to the wife of an alcoholic, but nothing could have prepared me for the shock wave, which ensued from a letter addressed to my husband from a friend who, strangely, lived nearby. To this day I do not know what possessed me to open this letter, but I did. In order to receive money for a job, my HUSBAND promised his friend I would have sex with his older and influential relative. When my husband failed to keep his promise, his friend wrote the letter, which I had opened. Imagine my utter disbelief that my husband had now become my pimp. Confronting my husband with the letter led to his emphatic denial.

The angrier I became, the louder I screamed, and the more I didn't care what consequences awaited me. I was beaten into submission until somehow, somewhere deep inside me, I mustered the courage to fight back with a rage I had never before experienced.

Suddenly, he stopped hitting and punching me and looked at me like a stranger. It was the very last time he raised his hand to me. I knew in that moment I must leave for my own safety and well-being. Thankfully, I was able to retreat to a friend's home for a few days. It was there that I decided it was time to share with my family the years of abuse at the hand of my abuser husband.

I was brought to tears at the outreach of love and support my family and friends offered when I confessed how much I had suffered. It had been so long since I was able to exhale and not worry that at any moment my life would be endangered. Never again would I have to return to a man who could lift a hand against me as my parents insisted that I stay with them and they would support in every way possible until I could get back on my feet.

The comfort and safety I felt lasted a couple of days before my husband appeared at the front door of my parent's home. He apologized profusely for his behavior, admitting he had a problem with alcohol and was willing to get the assistance he needed. With great reluctance, my father agreed to help him and arranged for admittance to a local hospital to begin a detox program for alcoholism.

After 12 days, he seemed to show signs of improvement and promised never to drink again. A few days after that, the promise was forgotten when the need for alcohol was satisfied with a purchase of his favorite brand. When I caught him, I confronted him with a promise I had made to myself — that the marriage was over, REALLY over! He didn't argue, or try to convince me that he would do better, instead he said, "I understand and I don't blame you."

On my way home that evening I was hit by a bus (yes, literally!) and rushed to the very hospital where my husband had received treatment for his alcoholism. Word traveled quickly and he appeared at my bedside, sheepish, apologetic and full of remorse. No amount of drugs used to ease my pain could alter the message in the metaphor; "hit by a bus." he was not to be trusted. His pleas for reconciliation fell on deaf ears, as I was resolute about my decision to divorce him.

After my discharge from the hospital, I returned to work. Shortly thereafter I was notified by the hospital that my husband fled from their facility leaving a suicide note behind. Somehow I refused to believe he would actually harm himself. A missing person's report was filed with the local police after family and friends conducted an exhaustive and unsuccessful search. The days turned into weeks, then the months into years. He had simply vanished, never to be seen or heard from again. I thought this would bring me some solace but it didn't.

Four years later, when I was ready to move forward in life, a lovely man and his six-year-old son who were visiting India from the U.S came into my life. I have been married to this man for the past 25 years. After moving to the U.S I decided to change careers from that of a school counselor to a psychotherapist as well as an alcohol and drug counselor. I was excited by life once again, but my happiness was short lived as I began experiencing similar emotions I had felt in my previous marriage.

Is this really happening to me? Unlike my abusive and uncaring first husband, my second husband was very loving and supportive, and despite this, I couldn't handle his love and caring for me. I was operating from a victim's mentality and consequently blamed him for my unhappiness.

I didn't believe I was worthy of love. He was trying his level best to keep me happy but it didn't make any difference as I continued to be angry and upset. His frustration at my inability to convey and receive love brought him to the breaking point. He talked of leaving me. I felt ashamed, guilty, and filled with worry and fear.

To save my marriage, I resolved to avoid getting into arguments, to be silent. As I slowly withdrew at home, I plunged into my career. Once again, an unhealthy set of circumstance cleared the path for self-abuse causing the physical, emotional and mental health challenges I was now experiencing.

Obtaining professional help only temporarily disarmed my feelings of being unworthy and undeserving. Sadly, my teenage stepson began acting out from the disharmony at home. We sought family counseling but it merely was a Band-Aid for the ever-increasing discord at home. So, of course, what there was to do was receive family therapy. Because the psychotherapy was not rendering long lasting results, I began looking for alternative healing methods.

Thank God I...® Am an Empowered Woman:

My journey to alternative healing modalities allowed me to realize that I must first heal my deep-seeded issues from the past before I could successfully create my future. My quest along this path of healing led me to a process called PSYCH-K®, which I discovered while reading Dr. Bruce Lipton's book, *The Biology of Belief*. It was to be the turning point for my husband, my stepson and me.

Were it not for the alcoholic man I married many years ago, I would not have learned that healing comes from within; it comes from what you have been taught to believe about yourself. I was the one abusing myself on the inside, which had me attracting abuse on the outside. Those lessons, indoctrinations or even whispers may have been ever so subtle, barely registering at the conscious level, but they were there.

I realized that at some level we all abuse ourselves. We all experience challenges and these challenges are there to push us to stand up for ourselves, set our own boundaries and grow. I realize my husband was loving and communicating with me the only way he knew how to at the time. I also see now that his actions pushed me, set the stage for me to decide how I would choose to be loved in the future. It also inspired me to help serve other people in learning how to control their destinies and appreciate themselves. Yes the pain from our lovers can indeed be brutal but full of effective life lessons.

Now, every aspect of my life is by design and I have the only say as to where the path will lead me. I take time to do what I love; spend time with the people I love. My journey has been riddled with challenges and pain, but I have crossed the Rubicon and can tell you, it feels fantastic! I am an empowered woman.

Awakening Your Inner Strength and Genius...

♥♥♥

With a commitment to supporting others in becoming free and empowered, I have been in private practice offering individuals and families the PSYCH-K® process in conjunction with other methods of healing I have perfected over the years. I am a certified addictions treatment specialist, Self-Actualization Coach and an instructor of PSYCH-K®.

P.S. My wonderful husband and I share an incredible life together of mutual love and respect. My stepson is a successful social worker making a difference with mentally challenged individuals. I have overcome addictive and compulsive behaviors and continue to move forward in life with confidence and hope!

To learn more about me visit my website:
RitaSoman.com

Thank God I Was Beaten Down
By Heather Vale Goss

SMACK!

The slap rang in my ears as much as it stung my face. My eyes burned as I fought back tears and stared at the ground so as not to accidentally make eye contact with my attacker. The man who had vowed to love me for better or for worse, in sickness and in health, till death do us part — my own husband.

I started to wish that death *would* do us part, sooner rather than later. How in the world had I gone from a confident, attractive woman to this quivering mess? From a victor to — as much as I hated to say it — a victim?

This was not part of my reality. Violence, yelling, daily putdowns, and the feeling of being entirely inadequate as a human being were all new to me. I had grown up with loving parents — maybe they didn't say or show it as often as they could, but they rarely yelled at me, almost never put me down, and certainly never hit me. They encouraged me to be my best, and I followed through by being a creative, artistic, straight-A student.

I went on to be a success in everything I put my mind to: an artist, a model, an actor, a TV show host, a writer, a radio reporter. With my creative skills, it seemed like everything I touched turned to gold. Maybe I stepped on a few toes on the way up the ladder, but at least nobody could ever say I didn't have drive or ambition. And I equated toughness with intelligence; I always said that if people were going to label me, I'd rather be a "bitch" than an "airhead."

"Hit me with your best shot," I'd say to life, ready to tackle any challenge. "I can take it!" Later I would embrace Bon Jovi, singing, "When the world gets in my face, I say, 'Have a nice day!'"

WHACK! WHACK! WHACK!

The blows kept coming from my husband. This time he smashed my head into the kitchen cupboard because I had called the 100% beef Angus franks he bought "hot dogs". That time he hammer-fisted the side of my head multiple times, leaving me with a grapefruit-sized goose egg and my hair matted together with blood.

He left me bleeding on the floor and walked out, and I was sure I was going to die. In fact, once again, I almost wanted to… except that there was a baby sleeping in the next room who needed me.

The world was in my face, but did I say, "Have a nice day?" Nope. That thought wasn't remotely part of my life anymore.

When he came back, he tried to make amends, and I thought it would be the last time he hit me. It wasn't… not by a long shot. By the time he hit me the final time, I had received repeated blows to my head over the period of several months — or was it several years? — until my memory began to be affected, and I had to ask him to only hit me below the neck. Then it was bruises all over my body for six months, to the point where I couldn't wear short sleeves, shorts, or go to the gym. Then summer rolled around, and I was chastised for letting my bruises show.

I told him I wasn't wearing long sleeves all summer, and if he didn't want people to see my bruises he had to stop hitting me. That lasted a month until he back fisted me so hard in the face that it split open, giving me a black eye and six stitches right below it.

That was the third time I called the cops, the second time he was charged, and the first time he was arrested.

Why was I going through these patterns? I dove deeply into my own past, trying to heal it so I could heal my present. I looked at how I had behaved with other people in the past — those who said I was snide or sarcastic, or insensitive, or full of myself.

Maybe the Universe was trying to knock some humility into me. But whatever was happening, I couldn't see it because I was running head first into so many trees that I completely lost sight of the forest.

I realized that while my parents had not put me down in the cruel ways my husband had, they had done so in subtle ways... something wasn't "done right" and something else was "supposed to be like this." I had gotten all A's except for one B... and instead of praising the overall effort, I heard "What happened in the class where you only got a B?"

I certainly didn't take it as abuse of any sort, and only hindsight let me see where they were lacking. They just didn't know how to build a child's self-esteem so the little being could grow up into a strong human who could take any blow — literal or figurative. And without that training and experience, I was floundering.

After that third visit from the cops, my husband was ordered to move out and not contact me. Of course, that didn't present a road block for him — simply a minor stumble. The assaults continued, but now they became verbal instead of physical. I was called every obnoxious name you can think of, including the ones that gentlemen would never call a woman.

And just like the blows had been mostly to my head, so were many of the insults: I was called every version of "stupid" that exists, including moron, imbecile, idiot and dumb, all with the F-word either before as an adjective, or after as a noun. Now I was being called both a bitch AND an airhead.

Every time I decided to let go and move on, I felt inspired. Then he would make contact again, sometimes apologizing wholeheartedly, and I'd be back in the snare again. It was such a typical cycle of domestic violence, although despite all the literature they threw at me, it took me a long time to recognize it... or maybe just to admit it to myself.

After all, it's hard to acknowledge being an abused spouse, a victim of domestic violence. That made me one of "them" — the women that, 20 years ago, I would have scoffed at, wondering why on earth they would stay with a man like that.

And on top of that shame, I kept trying to protect both him and myself. I was protecting him from himself — standing up for him, minimizing for him, making excuses for him — to my own detriment. Then I would protect myself from him, and try to run... only to realize that I could only do so at his expense.

I didn't fully pull myself out of the web of denial and shame until I finally decided I could only save him or me, realized in a flash of inspiration that it HAD to be me, and moved hundreds of miles away. Originally that move was supposed to happen together, "side by side, hand in hand and heart to heart," as our wedding vows had said.

But now I know that it could never be. And I recognized that all the insults to my intelligence were true, as long as I kept subjecting myself to abuse and tearing down my own boundaries as quickly as I put them up.

"You're married to a zebra. Why do you expect him to be anything but a zebra?" a wise friend once asked me. "Because maybe, just maybe, he's really a white horse," I had replied. After all, when we met, he had presented himself as my knight in shining armor. Maybe he truly was that white horse and was just painting on war paint and acting like a zebra for a while.

But no... I found out he had always been a zebra and had only dressed as a white horse at first.

When I finally let go of my dream, which had turned into a nightmare, I realized that it was never a nightmare at all. While it made me weaker for a long time, in the end it made me stronger. And while it made me sad and angry for a long time, in the end it brought me happiness and peace.

Now I know that I could never have been as strong as I am now, as confident as I am now, as aware as I am now, as compassionate as I am now, or as openly authentic as I am now if it hadn't been for my experiences with my husband.

And "till death do us part" didn't mean literal death... just the appropriate death of the fantasy, as all fantasies need to eventually die.

And a part of me died too... the old me that allowed all this to happen because I had lessons to learn and experiences to have. It was only by being beaten down that I was able to build myself back up, on my terms, like a phoenix rising from the ashes.

So while I don't have all the next steps in my life mapped out, I know that they involve connecting with people and helping them in ways that I wasn't equipped to do before. It took walking a mile (or 100) in the shoes of people I used to look down upon before I could realize the power in empathy and in my own inner strength.

Yes, as odd as it might sound, the challenges of being abused brought out both my gentle, sensitive, feminine side and my tough, strong, masculine side in a beautiful dance of yin and yang — proving that I didn't actually need a man in my life to be complete.

If what doesn't kill you makes you stronger, then I thank God that I didn't die when I thought it was my only way out... because if I had, I never would have known how powerful I could be and on so many levels.

Heather Vale Goss is a journalist, writer and interviewer who has worked in all media: TV, radio, print, and online. Known as The Unwrapper™, she focuses on unwrapping the secrets of success and discovery in personal development, entrepreneurship, art, health, and parenting. She works as a freelancer for top online publishers, including writing and conducting interviews for Thank God I.

Heather is also the author or co-author of several books, and you can view her multi-media portfolio at TheUnwrapper.com. Her personal blog, where she unwraps the mysteries of life, is at HeatherVale.com. When not working, she can often be found enjoying the Las Vegas sunshine with her son.

Thank God I Was Lost
By Ai Zhang

Tick tock, tick tock. The rhythmic clicking echoing from my wrist watch somehow became my entrance music, introducing me to the land of liberty. Twenty hours in a hard and sticky seat without any lower back support. Twenty hours of my wheels turning, cranking, and adjusting to my reality. I gained another day along with a new life, although an extra day seemed pointless, as lost as I was. China was my home, and the United States my future, which was ironic since I just came from the future. I stared out the window with no hint of a smile, leaving behind my culture and identity with the ever passing seas.

Turn the clock back twenty-four hours. There I was in Beijing, China, immersed in my ambivalence. I remember my parents' gaze. I remember his gaze. We were so serious, in love actually, and yet my education was just as important to me. I needed to make something of myself or, rather, find myself. It was the first and only time I saw my parents cry. As I walked into the airport they waved, and I looked back until they faded away. Tears ran down my face. The road ahead vanished, and all I could rely on was the saltiness of my tears.

Twenty-four hours later, I landed on U.S. soil. I was a foreigner in a foreign land. It felt like a dream from which I could not wake up. Faces swept past me in a blur. Even the air smelled exotic to me. My body was sleeping. My mind was drifting. How would I survive this unknown journey? I did not know. The uncertainty consumed me. I wanted to go home. I wanted my routine back. It may not have been my dream life, but at least I was comfortable with it.

From China to the U.S., it is not so much a geographical transformation as an identity transformation. I exposed myself to the unknown; and the unknown revealed the mysterious parts inside of me. I suspected that I embodied too much independence, at least in my parent's eyes and the eyes of Chinese society. But Americans welcomed my free-spirited nature. In fact, they encouraged it. I suppose I should have felt right at home, but somehow the essence of home did not exist anymore.

Was this the America, the Number One country that I had known from the mass media? Was this the place of my childhood dream? Was this the land of opportunity? My expectation of a magical place plummeted once reality crept in. My visions, dreams, and fantasies about the land of the free were so much better than what was in front of me. I realized that the U.S. wasn't everything I thought it would be.

"I am sorry... could you slow down and repeat what you were saying?" "Excuse me, I am lost, could you tell me how to get there?" "Could you give me a ride again? I don't drive." My shoulders drooped, my head hung low, and the corners of my mouth never seemed to rise. Forget about my ambitious dreams. I wanted to survive without being laughed at. This was a challenge, though, especially when someone would ask, "Hey Ai! What's up?" And my response would be to look up at the ceiling.

Every greeting became a chore. People in the United States are polite. In fact, people are too polite. It felt unreal. The very response "I'm doing great" indicated to me a tone of finality: "Please leave me alone... I am running late... I am too busy to care about you." As a foreigner, I wondered what was hidden behind the veil of politeness. Indifference, apathy, life crises, or what? Nonetheless, I embarked on a home-seeking quest even as I pondered whether I would ever feel at peace here.

I longed for intimate, interpersonal relationships and the lack of those increased the yearning for my loved ones. I missed my boyfriend. He desperately wanted to join me but his VISA had been rejected. We emailed each other frequently and exchanged words of affection. We also fought just as often. He suggested marriage several times, but I could never say the word "yes." I desired his embrace, I thought, but maybe I actually yearned for the world to open its arms to me. My mother said he didn't love me enough, that he had ulterior motives, but my heart wasn't prepared to let go of the past quite yet.

Even as my mind turned on in my classes, my heart remained across the sea. Speaking up and being noticed were accepted here but I greatly disliked doing both. Nor did I enjoy maintaining eye contact. These practices are not common in my home country. I avoided standing out — at least I tried — but inevitably experienced the opposite by not knowing common mannerisms and idioms. But as long as I wasn't asked to speak publicly, I figured I could get by. That's when I received the news. In order to maintain my scholarship at Syracuse, I was required to teach a public speaking class.

Twenty-four pairs of eyes locked in on me. Their expressions penetrated through me like electrical currents. I stood before a public speaking class. My mind went blank. Time stopped. I could hear nothing but my shaking voice and beating heart. What about my accent? My limited knowledge of American culture? My inability to make jokes and maintain eye contact? I wore my fear and embarrassment like a heavy coat. I don't remember how I managed to survive that first day. Yet, I recall each and every student looking at me in a familiar way, as if I were transparent. How did they know that I questioned my identity?

Thank God for summer. I headed back to China... back to my friends, my parents, and my love. A touch of heaven warmed my heart as he wrapped his arms around me. I was home. Home. Accepted, protected, and loved. Then why did the feeling of uncertainty still exist within me? The consistency of life in my homeland certainly comforted me. My parents continued to voice their opinions regarding my decision-making. The fighting and making up resumed with my boyfriend. For my birthday, he presented me with a beautiful necklace, and he brought up our future as he so often did. I listened and partially believed him as China and America continued their tug-o-war within me.

Then my summer vacation was over. I found myself staring at my books, attempting to mentally prepare myself for the second year of my master's program. I started to feel that old magnetic pull towards home — but this time it was New York that was my home. I knew I hadn't fulfilled my dreams, nor did I feel at ease in my new surroundings. But as I said goodbye to my boyfriend, I knew he would not be a part of my future. My heart returned to its rightful owner. I never spoke to him again.

I felt myself shutting down; slipping away. I was alone, forced to uncover my authentic self. But where was it hiding? I desperately needed to escape. Hearing Chinese music, looking at the picture of my parents, thinking about... time to leave. As much as I avoided crying, nothing could have stopped those tears from making a dramatic exit. Releasing my repressed emotions was a relief but almost too much to bear. Distraction, distraction, I needed a distraction.

Thank God I...® Am an Empowered Woman:

After wandering around campus awhile, I noticed a seminar being held in one of our lecture halls. The topic discussed was death, but I didn't mind; at least I could mope with similar company. At first, her occasional glances ceased to faze me, but then she rose from her seat and started walking my way; my heart rate increased, I tried to act normal, but kept shifting around nervously. She was an older woman with kind eyes who set me at ease once she sat down next to me and smiled warmly. After exchanging a few superficial words about our lives, she paused, tilted her head, and looked at me with the deepest concern. "Why are you here?"

The blank sheets of paper were stacked in front of me with the tip of my pen tracing the lines, impatiently waiting for the words to flow out of me. I desperately wanted to express myself, but the need to control stood in my way. Why are you here? Her question echoed in my mind. I did not know the answer but was determined to find out. I took a deep breath, slowly exhaled, and began to free write. Hours later, the pages were filled, my hand was aching, and my spirit was rejuvenated.

Why am I here? It was as if I had manifested my guardian angel, pointing me to look in the opposite direction.

All this time, the choices, the fear of people, the uncertainty on the outside overshadowed something so much more profound. By contemplating why I was here, I began a road to answer life's most important question, "Who am I?" and I would find my way.

I realized I was more than the emotions that challenged me. By writing it all out, I began to put the pieces of my life together, and I began to see I was many things. It became clear that I was Chinese and I was American, and that I needed the experience of both in order to connect deep in my spirit and with others as a human being with value. By looking into this woman's kind eyes and being present with 'Why am I here?' I began the road to discovering who I was. This question guided me towards a moment of grace that opened my eyes to a much wiser me.

I felt guided, and this is what helped empower me to appreciate my challenging road, and helped me ask more profound questions. From that day forward, as my emotions came up I had a beacon to look deeper inside.

My hopelessness slowly disappeared and was replaced with a new zest for life. Perhaps I was meant to be this woman all along, not bound by one society's perspective on how I should behave, but a person who embraces everything around her without feeling guilty about it.

Thank God I was lost because it opened up my heart to embrace the unknown and expand the frontier of my being. It opened the door of spirituality for me and led me to new experiences like joining a mediation club where I met the man I would fall in love with, marry, and celebrate the birth of our precious son. I no longer feel imprisoned by my home-searching journey in a foreign land because I found my home... it existed deep within me all along. I no longer have to choose between my Chinese heritage and my American life. I can have them both and love them both. My authentic self is a complex web of two, dominating cultures fused together, forming an intricate pattern of various angles, risk and discovery; yet, I am free.

As a native Chinese, Ai Zhang came to the United States in the summer of 2003 to further her education. She obtained

Thank God I... ® *Am an Empowered Woman:*

her MA and PH.D. degrees in Communication respectively from Syrcuse University and the University of Maryland. She currently serves as an assistant professor at a liberal arts college called Richard Stockton College of NJ.

Thank God I Gave Custody of My Kids to My Ex-Husband
By Alice Cablayan

The room was dark as I awoke suddenly and sat straight up in a strange bed. It was between one and two in the morning, and I could see the beams of light from the street lamps streaming into the room. I looked straight ahead of me at the blinds that covered the windows facing the parking lot.

"The parking lot," I whispered to myself as I shook my head in regret.

I began thinking about the beautiful hillside view from my bedroom windows on the second floor of my large three bedroom house. The large, magenta bougainvillea I planted three years ago was now large enough to grace the terrace of the back patio. The Devic Kingdom of plants enchanted me — the bougainvillea blossoms reached out to me at my window and twinkled flower fairies vying for my attention. I basked in the sweet silence of the memory until the pain in my heart brought me abruptly back to the present moment. A frown furrowed in my brows. I had traded my magical hillside view for one of parked cars and street lamps in a crowded condominium parking lot.

As I continued to sit in the dimly lit bedroom, I reached out to touch the outline of the brass daybed frame, that lay smothered against the wall. It was cold, impersonal, and unwelcoming, so very different from the warm, cherry wood headboard I was accustomed to admiring and polishing on my own bed. The accompanying mattress was worse. It was uncomfortable thin, lumpy, worn and faded, it was a rude contrast from the plush king-sized bed I'd slept in just twenty four hours ago.

As my body struggled to be comfortable, the wires beneath the mattress squeaked like a bed in a run-down motel from a ghetto drug scene in a movie. I shuddered at the thought of who slept here before me and what might have taken place. I pulled my knees up to my chest as the strange silence of the night began to cruelly mock me with its dark emptiness.

"Oh God... what have I done?" I whispered painfully to myself. I buried my face in my hands as the tears formed and rolled down from my eyes and onto my cheeks. "Oh, no... . Oh, no..." I said to myself as the stark, cold realization of my decision began to settle in on me. My breathing began to heave and jerk, and I had to hold my breath to control the convulsions that wanted to release itself through my tears. My heart began breaking and shattering into tiny, crystal-clear sharp chards as I felt an invisible sword cut into the depths of my soul.

"WHAT HAVE I DONE???" I said to myself in exasperation. I began to weep from the depths of my Soul. My throat uncontrollably moaned like the ghost of a wandering banshee and the flow of my breathing was interrupted with jerked movements as I struggled to control my breath.

To soothe myself, I began to rock my body back and forth. I clutched my knees to my chest to relieve the grief that my body and emotions ached to release. I wanted to cry, but I felt afraid to; for I knew that my cry would be no ordinary cry. I knew that deep down inside of me my primordial self was in deep, raw pain — angry at the circumstances that caused me to cut away the bonds of mother and child before its time.

No, this would be no ordinary cry, and I did not know if I was ready to meet the destroyer part of myself- the great dark goddess known as Kali-Ma in India. The cry of this inner goddess would be the wail of an angry animal separated from her young. I was afraid of her life and the fruit of her womb — her two young children.

Like warriors on horseback racing downhill to attack their enemies, feelings of guilt began invading my inner world. I hugged my knees to my chest to comfort the achy feeling I experienced deep in my gut. Suddenly, a thought entered my mind. "They're crying now — wondering where I'm at, looking for me in the dark of my bedroom and seeing that all of my stuff is gone," I quietly whispered to myself.

I closed my eyes and felt a sharp, cold pain cut through my solar plexus. Was this a physical pain? No. Yet it felt as if I had performed Hara-Kiri, the ancient Japanese ritual of honorable suicide.

The thought of my children made me realize that I woke up from my sleep because I intuitively felt them crying out for me. I could feel the screams of their distress, and in my mind's eye, I could see them weeping with a look of shock and bewilderment that their mother was suddenly gone from their home. I could see my tiny daughter's eyes filled with tears that ran down her small, brown cheeks, and I could see my small four year-old son holding and comforting her - telling her that everything will be ok even though he, too, could not make sense of the confusion he was feeling. In my mind, I could also see their father, bewildered in his own hurt and anger of my having left them, all of them while trying to bring order to the hysteria occurring in his house. The vision was too much for me to bear. I shut my eyes and willed myself to block any more psychic impressions from coming in to my inner sight and to my inner feelings.

Ironically, the darkness of my room was a comfort from the light of truth. Thoughts of self-judgment with accusations of being a bad mother began playing in my mind like a broken record. "How could I forgive myself?" I thought. "How selfish was I? How could I leave them and just think of myself like this? Feeling numb and uncertain, I wondered if I had done the right thing.

I knew in my heart that I'd imposed a trauma on them that they would have to live with and work out for the rest of their lives. Thoughts of negative future fantasies began to swirl in my mind of my grown children as young adults having personality issues and problems — of being overly needy in relationships or worse, numbing their pain through substance abuse or other forms of addiction. "No . . . NO!" I firmly told myself. "No . . . don't you think like that!"

I had to remember. I had to think back to the reasons WHY I did this in the first place. WHY I left a beautiful suburban home and left my role as a wife and full-time mother — WHY I left a garden I lovingly cultivated and two small dogs I loved and cherished as my animal guardians. In this place of darkness, I had to remember the light of my self-loving and remind myself of the reasons WHY I chose to give the rightful care of my children to their father. I wondered WHY I had the belief that I couldn't take care of them myself.

I felt that my comfortable world of homemaking and suburbia crumbled before me like the ruins of Pompeii. Lost in my thoughts of self-judgment and pity, my bed squeaked as I adjusted my weight from hugging my knees. While trying to make myself comfortable, my eyes caught a small ray of light that reflected off of a small silver-plated picture frame that contained a picture of my children. I reached over to the nightstand, grabbed the picture, and looked at the softness of my children's eyes through the cold and impersonal glass that protected their image. "I'm sorry," I said aloud to their smiling faces in the picture.

"Mommy's sorry she had to leave you," I continued. My nose sniffed as tears began to well up in my eyes. "But you'll be ok . . . I promise," I said, secretly hoping that my promise to them would hold true over the years. I continued to speak to them lovingly, and I held the picture of them in my hand as if I were holding their tender faces for the last time. I took a deep breath in and held it for a few seconds as I gathered the courage inside of me to explain why I did not say goodbye to them in person.

"Mommy had to go. I wanted to say goodbye to you and explain why I had to leave so suddenly, but your daddy would not let me say good-bye. He thought it best that I just leave. I didn't agree with him but when I came back to the house to say good bye and get my things, he sent both of you away for the day so that I would not be able to see you. It broke my heart not to properly say good-bye to both of you. I know you don't understand right now, and I know this hurts a lot. But I want you to know that even though I am not with you at home, I am with you in your heart." Their sweet faces just stared back at me; their expressions frozen in my memory. If only I could hold their soft cheeks in my hands and press them against my beating heart one last time. Thoughts of self-preservation began to swirl in my heart and mind. As a full time homemaker, I had not worked in eight years and I desperately needed to find a job so that we could be together again. Money in my wallet meant having a home and providing a better life for my children. It tore me up inside to not have them near me, but I hoped with everything in me that they would understand why I couldn't provide for them at the time. I desired their happiness above all and knew that my husband could give them a nice home to live in. My eyes moved from their tender smiles to the window, where I contemplated their future.

In their current situation, they had access to the best schools, safe neighborhoods filled with their friends, and so much love and support from my in-laws. I wanted more for them... more than I had ever received growing up. If only their father and I didn't fight so much...I knew it negatively impacted our children, and I did not wish to expose them to it anymore. They needed to hold on to the happy memories for now until it was time to make new memories of us three altogether.

As a mother, though, how do you tell your own children that it's better to move out and stay away for a while? I ran my fingers over the photo. Again I attempted to explain myself, "You see, mommy felt like she was dying inside, and in order for me to still be around and be your mommy, I had to leave the fighting. I know this is hard to understand right now, and it will be lonely for a while, but Mommy has to go away to take care of herself so that she can take care of you. Just know that I will always, always love you."

And with that, I closed my eyes and said a small prayer for the long journey that lay ahead of all of us. I bowed my head and gave thanks to God that even though I didn't know what my next step was, I knew that my kids would be taken care of and that somehow I would be alright.

Alice Cablayan is a writer, spiritual teacher, singer, musician, and business administrator who inspires people through her intuitive sense of compassion and her funny, direct, no-nonsense approach to living a practical spiritual life.

Having studied energy healing with Del Pe, Master Sage and consultant to world leaders as well as prayerful group spiritual service with The Aetherius Society, she brings her share of Heaven to Earth as a light bearer, healer and singer through heart-felt songs, mantra, and sound healing. As a writer, her article in the Huffington Post entitled, "The Law of Compassion vs. The Law of the Land - The custody case of Veronica Capobianco" brought national awareness for the need of compassion when transitioning custody of children under the Indian Child Welfare Act of 1978. The Veronica Capobianco case went all the way to the Supreme Court.

Alice has a B.S. in Business Management and an M.A. in Spiritual Psychology from the University of Santa Monica. You can learn more about Alice by visiting her website: www.sageadvicebyalice.com

Thank God I Stood Up For Myself
By Denise Gladwell

I moved to an island paradise to begin a new chapter in my life and to be with a man I had fallen in love with while on vacation there. I had envisioned an idyllic life filled with happiness, romance, excitement and fun in the sun. Less than a year later I would be broken and battered; physically, emotionally, and mentally.

I had just come through a time of great loss and thought a trip to visit an old friend in the Cayman Islands would be the ticket to rejuvenate and heal myself.

My friend's roommate and I instantly hit it off. We formed a friendship that quickly turned into a romance. Our connection was very intense. He was sweet and romantic, singing me love songs and preparing candlelit dinners. We talked about a future together and I fell totally in love.

Within months I had found a job, packed up my house and relocated myself.

Almost immediately after I arrived he became controlling and abusive. He insisted that he should make all of the decisions in my life - how I dressed, who I socialized with, everything I did. He'd bring up mistakes from my past that I'd confessed to him; throwing them in my face, "There can be only one driver in a relationship and obviously YOU aren't capable!"

There had been red flags and warnings of his Jekyll & Hyde personality before, but I had always made excuses for him and wrote them off. I ignored what my intuition was telling me.

He would suddenly become unreasonable and start arguments over the smallest things. If I tried to stand up for myself or argue back, he became physically abusive.

For days afterward he would cry and apologize, promising it would never happen again and begging me not to leave him. He would be sweet and romantic for a while; but then it would happen again.

I knew I should leave, but was conflicted. I loved this man and I wanted to help him. I mistakenly thought I could "love him better." I was living in paradise but going through hell.

On New Year's Eve we went out with a couple he knew who were visiting the island. We were all dressed up and enjoyed a great dinner and champagne at midnight. It was a fun evening. On the way home he started in on me.

"What did you say to my friends about me?"

"What do you mean? I didn't say anything negative about you."

"Don't give me that crap. Tell me what you said!"

"I didn't say anything."
"You're lying. She said something to me about the way I treat you. What did you say?"

"I have no idea what you're talking about."

And so on — all the way home.

Thank God I... ® *Am an Empowered Woman:*

We got to my house; I got out of the car and told him to leave. He refused and followed me. I opened my front door and suddenly, I felt my feet give way as he violently shoved me into the house. I landed hard, the wind knocked out of me. I struggled to find my breath and to get up, but he kept knocking me down, over and over again. My knees and elbows smashing on the tile again and again as he kicked me, slammed me into walls and pummelled me with his fists. I couldn't think of anything, but instinctively trying to protect myself and escaping. I was beyond terrified.

At one point I was able to get out the front door, but he grabbed at me as I was fleeing; catching me by my hand and twisting violently. White-hot pain shot through my hand and I buckled to my knees. He dragged me back into the house and it continued - for hours.

His cruelty knew no bounds. He slammed me into a door frame so hard that it shattered; he pinned me on the bed and jumped on me until I was sick to my stomach. "Please stop, you're going to kill me" I said weakly, while lying on the bathroom floor. I didn't have the strength left to scream or try to defend myself anymore, and I knew that I was badly injured. I don't know what made him stop, at that point, but thankfully he did. The next day I awoke; my arm broken in two places, two broken fingers and so bruised and sore that I could hardly move.

I underwent months of painful physiotherapy and had surgery to correct the damage to one of my fingers. Physically, I will never heal completely, but the emotional injuries were much deeper and more profound. I struggled with the physical and emotional damage done by this man and my strong desire to forgive him. After all he had done to me, I still wanted to see the good in him and to help him.

About a year later, a girl contacted me and told me that she had just gotten out of a relationship with him. She wanted to talk to me. We met and I listened in horror as she told me that he had assaulted her multiple times as well. The tale she told mirrored my own, sometimes word for word. I listened to her story, hearing my own experience in her relationship with him. She told me about how kind he had been in the beginning, how sincere, and then how ugly and abusive he had become.

I recognized that I had been part of his pattern all along. I wasn't his last victim and, I was willing to bet, I wasn't his first either.

"He's going to end up killing some poor woman one day!" I thought to myself, feeling sick.

"I'm pressing charges against him," she said to me.

I knew that I should charge him as well. I felt that it was important that the police and/or courts know that this was a pattern of behaviour for him. But I was terrified of the ramifications and of what he might do to me in retaliation.

I met with a lot of opposition from family and friends over the decision to press charges. This was out of love and concern for me. They were afraid for my safety and didn't want me to go through the trauma of a court case – "just put it behind you and go on with your life."

Part of me wanted to heed their advice and take the easy way out. The bigger part of me knew that I could not live with myself if he hurt or killed someone and I had done nothing to prevent it. I realized that the right thing to do and the easy thing to do are not always the same thing.

I had loved this man and had never wanted to do anything to hurt him or ruin his life. Although it broke my heart, I pressed charges. That was the point when I finally stopped being his victim.

The court case took almost two years to resolve. It took another year for him to serve his time and to be deported. Those years were difficult, painful and terrifying. But, they were also a time of coming to terms, of healing and of learning. They were a time of gaining wisdom and recognizing my own strength.

I learned a great deal about the power of forgiveness; for your own sake, no one else's, and having gratitude – for it all.

The lesson I want people to take from my story is to pay attention to your red flags. My intuition was telling me all along to run. I chose to ignore it because I didn't want to believe what it was telling me. If I had listened, I would be telling you a very different story.

Trust your feelings, gut instincts and inner guidance – they're there for a reason; they're there to protect you. Your inner voice is your connection to your higher power and your innate wisdom. It's the voice of your soul and the angels who watch over you.

You have to love and take care of *yourself* first and foremost. Be your own guardian. Don't sacrifice yourself for love; if you have to it's not love. You can't love someone better and you can't change someone.

Ask for help when you need it. It's there if you just reach out for it. There are others, who have been through the same thing, have survived it and who will understand. You are stronger than you think you are and you are not alone.

Denise Gladwell lives in the Cayman Islands where she has built a life that she loves. Through healing from this experience, she has learned much, most importantly the power of gratitude, forgiveness, and letting your past make you better, not bitter.

Thank God I Recognized the Blessing in The Crisis
By Dr. Marcia Becherel

Maybe my father was right. Maybe I shouldn't have married him. But we had such a great relationship... I thought. Ten years of marriage flew by because of our connection, our similar interests, and our thirst for knowledge. I was a successful medical doctor and scientist, while he was a scientist and University professor. We lived a life of routine, but accepted it with no complaints. When we bought our house 3 years ago, I believed that we completed the fairy-tale picture. The white picket fence may not have existed; however, the smiles, the laughs, our finances, and the love were all in abundance. Our marriage equaled perfection, in fact, our lives did as well.

Then came that day when the rain was so intense it beat against the windows like a native tribe beats the drums to warn the people that danger is near. The front door creaked a bit when he came home, making the extreme weather ever so present. He walked cautiously towards me, his gaze directed at the floor, hiding the truth in his eyes. I just sat there and stared aimlessly at our white walls. Why hadn't we painted them yet? Wow, that coffee table is dusty. Why did we buy that bookshelf again? Why did my husband fall in love with another woman? I heard the words, but images of us kept flashing through my mind.

We both had the ability to be sneaky. When we first started dating, we hid it from my family. I wanted our relationship out in the open, but I knew they would never accept him because he wasn't Chinese. The truth always manages to surface though, and my suspicions of their reaction came to fruition. "Break up with him or you are not part of this family anymore!" my father barked. I grew weary of the ultimatums and knew that leaving my boyfriend was not an option. My choice resulted in them disowning me. Somehow I found the courage to stay strong, and with what little composure I had left, I packed my bags and left the nest.

Although my mother did not support my relationship, she certainly didn't want to see me go. She begged my father to open up his heart and allow me back into the family. In his mind, I had greatly disrespected him, which in Chinese culture is one of the worst things a child can do to his or her parents. My mother continued to persuade him and to view the situation through my eyes. I don't know how she managed to change his mind, but he reluctantly gave in... eventually. He learned to accept it, especially after we got married. Besides, my husband was family now — a permanent fixture in our home.

The sound of an incoming text popping up on his phone startled me. The white walls stared at me once more, and the news he just shared with me suddenly appeared in bold, black font as if on an old projector with the sound of the reel turning in the background. I saw my life projected on the wall, scene after scene, flashing and flickering like strobe lights at a rave.

Who cares about the color of the walls now? They started closing in on me at this point, and my husband was no longer there to save me. My body began to tingle and then a feeling of numbness washed over me. I tried to move. I tried to speak. But I was caught in one of those nightmares where you attempt to yell or run but it becomes absolutely impossible to do either. I was paralyzed but at the same time felt my blood boiling. Heis eyes scanned my entire body like a laser in one of those airport scanners, searching intensely for any hidden weapons. I certainly shot him dagger eyes.

"What?" Suddenly my senses returned and my mouth opened briefly to ask a cliché question that really wasn't going to explain his behavior but only reiterate his piercing truth. Instead of letting him try to create a weak explanation, the panic set in, and the ranting began. "My parents have moved back to Taiwan, my sister is in the U.S., and my two brothers are in Australia! I'll be all alone... in Brazil."

My heart beat faster and my breathing intensified as I searched for comfort, hope, or someone to hold me and tell me that the sun would shine again. His excuses were irrelevant at this point. No one ever wants to believe this will happen to them, and I certainly never thought it would happen to me. All of the sacrifices I made to marry him seemed to lack meaning now.

My world turned dark, empty and cold; each moment was filled with questions that led to blatant dead ends. I fell deeper and deeper into the darkest part of myself, searching for any speck of light. I sought truth, resolution, and recovery for what I had lost; truth from him, resolution from within, and recovery from above.

My requests remained unanswered, which only aggravated me further but solidified my reality. His words strangled me and kept me immobile, as if stuck in a painting with a vast view in sight, but permanently positioned with one expression and no voice. Maybe that's what I needed to learn, to discover and embrace my true self. His decision to love another woman forced me to embark on a new voyage, headed straight for the unknown.

During my quest, I found something unexpected... something buried deep within me, hidden for years. At first, I did not recognize the still small voice that tugged at my heart. It was easier to ignore the yearning instead of meditate on possibility. Self-pity guarantees a bleak future, which I assumed was my sentence. I had definitely reached a breaking point. I saw myself wading in a well, clinging to anything that might resurface me and pull me toward the sun. Why is it that crisis brings out your potential?

The fighter... the believer that always existed within my spirit but remained dormant for so long, finally arose, but with a vengeance this time. Gratitude began to flow through my veins like honey in a bee hive, providing me nourishment and strength. The realization that tomorrow held promise suddenly hit me like a ton of bricks. The light switch stared back at me awaiting my touch; the answer was right in front of me the whole time. Life is amazing, when we recognize the blessing in the crisis.

It was painful, of course, but we didn't fight — we have actually stayed good friends! Recognizing that the divorce offered us a second chance at life eliminated the need to blame and hold grudges. I know who I am and what I'm made of thanks to my ex-husband.

The door may have closed on that relationship, but that allowed for another one to open. I fell in love again and have been happily married for 14 years. Now I am in a new adventure, sharing a beautiful and amazing journey of personal evolution with my husband that would not have been possible if I was still in my first marriage. I remember an old lady telling me when I had to choose between my family and my ex-husband: "No matter what you do just make sure that if one day your husband leaves you, you can stand up on your own and continue your journey with a smile on your face." Thank God I did.

Dr. Marcia Becherel is Co-Founder & CEO of Mastery to Success — The Human Potential Academy, a coaching and training institute dedicated to empower people to discover and realize their full potential and live a magnificent life. Marcia has a solid foundation in Science and Medicine with a Medical Degree, a PhD, and over 26 years of experience in Cell Biology and Research. However, Marcia found her life purpose in the Mind Body Connection and personal transformation. Marcia is also the co-author of "Relationship Equation: The Art and Science of Creating Fulfilling Relationships" and "Farewell to Anxiety: 7 Quick & Simple Steps to Rid Yourself of Anxiety!"

Today Marcia teaches principles she uses herself to help people connect with their heart, reveal the magnificence of their true self, and live a meaningful and fulfilling life.

www.masterytosuccess.com.au

Thank God I Was Abused
By Adele Green

I woke up to the smell of hot butter on toast. I loved visiting Granny's house. I was a curious child with blond hair and red cheeks. "If you ask why one more time," Granny used to say. She taught me how to read before I went to school. One day I discovered a beautiful story about a man that gave his life for those he did not know. This act of kindness fascinated me for I never knew that kind of love. As I continued reading the Children's Bible, my 6-year-old heart melted, and I wept. Since I was alone, I immediately knelt down, closed my eyes (like my granny and granddad use to do) and prayed. "Jesus, I give you my heart."

"It stays our secret," he whispered. I hated his hot breath on my face as he slowly traced my skin with his fingertips. I was only 11, but understood that my step dad's behavior was inappropriate. But the children of my culture in my neighborhood never questioned authority figures. Saying no cost me dearly, he would have terrible mood swings and made sure I knew it was my fault my family members were being treated harshly.

I remember looking up at the night sky from my little town in South Africa, asking Jesus if he heard my prayers. Reading storybooks helped me escape my pain, but only on a temporary basis. The truth was that my life did not resemble that of all the happy children I read about and envied. Every night he came home, my heart sank as it usually meant that we would have our "special time" together. I told myself it was my fault, being pretty and wearing revealing clothes; shorts must have been too tempting for him.

My mother refused to believe me. I had endured his abuse for five years and finally found the courage to share my secret with her. Unable to support me, she did the best she could and told him what I had said. He played the part of the innocent father figure so well. I don't know if she feared him or financial disaster more, but nothing came of being vulnerable by telling my mother.

Who could I turn to next? I wrote a letter to school principal to ask to live at the hostel. But, it was two years until the school councilor finally removed my sister and me from our home. Our family abandoned us. The minister of the church I frequented five days a week came to the hostel and told me to stop telling lies. I had trusted him as the representative of God, he represented who and what I loved the most; but where was Jesus now? I couldn't take it any longer and since Jesus had forgotten about me, I decided to forget about him. The tears streamed down my red cheeks for weeks as I let go of everything that I knew. My mother said she would come for us, but she never did.

Why was God rejecting me? Why was my own mother rejecting me? I used to ponder these questions. Maybe she had a similar story to tell but never could or perhaps, my biological father committing suicide but trying to make it look like my mother killed him caused her to dislike me. I was told that he loved me like no other, and maybe she resented that. The hardest part was that I could never talk about it and she could never remember any of it.

I was lost, numb, and broken. I shut down and only let people see what I wanted them to see. Wearing a layer of protection decreased my chances of being disappointed or hurt. But I was hurting deep down inside... so much so that I found it difficult to breathe at times and make it through the day. So I made a vow to God. "Please Lord, if you take this away, I will do anything for you." And then God and I both forgot about it... or so I thought.

That's when I met my husband. He noticed the real me beyond the mask I wore for the world. I was finally loved for my true self. God had heard me this time and sent me an angel. He was so easy to love, and I opened up my heart completely to him for the 3 years we were married. Then he left this earth. The cancer had spread, and after an 18 month battle, he lost. I was once again alone at 27.

Even though I eventually remarried and had two boys, my busy life never let me forget how lonely I felt inside. My projection of looking for God in men made it impossible to be satisfied. I became deeply depressed and started working again, hoping that a job could provide the distraction. The outside God I made promises to became a distant memory. But I was to be surprised by life yet again. At 36, frustrated with corporate power play and disillusioned with the demands of motherhood, I resigned from work with nothing to do and took a sabbatical from the real world. I needed to find out where I really belonged. During that final week of my formal employment, I received news that my step dad had shot himself and died.

I didn't know what to think of the news at first. I never had the chance to tell him how much he affected my life. I turned my back on Jesus because of what he did to me. He obviously had his own demons to battle, who eventually won. Maybe he decided to end his life over the pain he caused my mother and me. Who knows exactly? I began to cry for the first time after so many years.

Realizing that we have all made mistakes but that misfortune can lead to a reawakening helped me to forgive myself and to stop judging my past and enter the journey of living consciously with pain.

A sense of clarity washed over me like a sun bath. I could let them go now... all of them. Their perfectly framed faces appeared before my eyes and as I studied each one, I no longer felt my body cringe, nor did I want to curl up in the fetal position. I simply turned the pictures over and brushed them aside.

Now I trusted myself to provide all the love I needed to be a fulfilled human being. The loss and the rage transcended into joy about the permanent presence of what I define as God for me in my life. What was my tragedy became my gift to the world by sharing what I could not as a child.

Today I thank God for growing up in Africa, in a culture that is not tolerant of giving children a voice, so I can speak up for myself and take my power back consciously. Thank God I was violated and did not know it until I was eleven so that I could transcend the shame of secrecy into a personal relationship with myself, leaving me content with the perfect moments to appreciate moments of pure joy. Thank God my first husband died so I could learn about judgment and living in the moment accepting what happened to me without expecting my partners to do it for me.

Thank God I searched all my life to find what I was looking for inside of me. An aha moment happens in our minds, but a heart connection sets us free from the illusion that we are stuck in our circumstances when we experience ourselves as perfect in that moment and feel the compassion for ourselves that God has for us. I live moment by moment, connecting to my own desires and living in touch with my purpose. Touching lives as a kinesiology-coach, I create awareness about staying connected with your heart and mind.

I finally found my way back to my first love... the One I stumbled upon at Granny's house. The smell of hot butter on toast filled the air again, and I could feel my childhood innocence reenter my soul. Someone once told me that the sun comes up for everyone, but we only see the beauty of the sunrise when it is alive inside of us. In those moments life is perfect because we notice it. But even when we don't notice its magnificence, it is still unconsciously perfect. In the end I found what I was looking for, which was right here in my heart... the greatest gift ever... the LOVE that I am and always have been but could not notice until now.

Adelé Green is a published author, keynote speaker and a poet. She writes for South African traditional media. She is active on social media, which lead to her latest project, a new subscription blog site called <u>NakedWithAdele.com</u>. It supports her new book "Can You See Me Naked? Grow in a Conscious Relationship," written especially for men about women.

Thank God for Online Dating
By Christine Little

Another Saturday night, I just finished a yoga class with several elderly women in my small town in the Western Carolina Mountains. So much for my social life.

Whoopee, it's 9:30 pm, and I'm home alone again. "Get brave, get online," I said to myself. "No one is looking over your shoulder; you don't have to tell anyone what you are doing; besides you can create a new persona!" A few clicks was all it took and voilà, a whole new world of single people unfolded. Wow! I used to think it was fun to shop by number at the local tri-athlete competitions, but this was even more exciting! I loved reading the profiles, looking at the pictures, examining snippets of peoples" lives. At the same time, I had this gnawing aching fear of saying anything, at the risk of being rejected. I had this fear of not being "good enough" almost my entire life.

Let the games begin! I was not aware at the time how this event would change my thinking. I found it somewhat challenging to write my profile. The questionnaire part was easy; it was a checklist. Now for the words... What information would I want someone to know about me? How could I spark interest? Where's my thesaurus? This was it; I was finally putting myself out there. Not good enough? Good enough for what!

LittleDoll

Frisky, funny, witty, sultry, I enjoy old love songs, Tony Bennett, Sinatra. Love to shoot trap and sporting clay, love a challenge. Honesty is important to me. High heels and hiking boots, leather and lace, black tie or BBQ, versatility and patience, prankster and nurturer, book worm and Barbie doll.

Looking for a man who appreciates intelligence and who can laugh at himself and knows the art of kissing. Be non-judgmental, compassionate, caring, can cook breakfast or make a great cup of coffee. Someone who enjoys fine wine and candlelit dinners, soft music, jazz, blues, traveling.

Dog lover, horseback riding or motorcycles. I love romance, flowers, surprise me...

I sent it in for approval and within 24 hours, I was officially single and ready to mingle in the online dating world. Wow, I got mail!! That was fast! I was pleased to have so many responses without a picture. Little did I realize that people can have new profiles automatically sent to them, nonetheless, it was a great ego stroke, and my ego was in withdrawal! I had been alone for a few years, and my confidence level had dropped below zero. So it was nice to have some attention. Two days later I put up a photo, something flirty and sexy. Bam! I was hit with 30 emails. It's true, men are visual creatures!

It felt like an interview process. Applications for my company. While my stomach turned at the fear of being humiliated, what a great way to view potential mates quickly and decide which ones I would like to speak with. Using the many safeguards of course, like meeting in public places, never giving out personal numbers or emails, even my last name. Making it to the first date was tricky. I found that speaking on the phone saved a lot of time and hurt feelings. I could sense levels of desperation immediately. As I began to listen to other people and study them, I became more and more comfortable in my own skin. Eventually I even started to get good at it!

I perfected the fine art of flirting. When not to respond, stay in or get out of my own comfort zone, how to let people know I'm not interested without hurting their feelings. It seemed like when I responded with a simple "Thank you for the compliment," the receiver took it as an opportunity to pounce. I was being patient and particular.

There was one man of particular interest I referred to as The Big Kahuna from Maryland. He and I played phone tag for several days before connecting. I'm at the grocery store when I get a call, and he says he just came in from the vineyard. Now that's interesting, I said, "I'm standing in the wine yard of Harris Teeter!" Wow, a man after my heart owns a vineyard. Our first meeting was in Charlotte, he was on a business trip. We decided to meet for dinner.

Funny to meet someone in person for the first time and feel as if you have known them forever, that's how comfortable I was. We had a fun evening of laughter and conversations of the adventures we'd had. He was a very interesting man who grew up on a vineyard in France as a child and had traveled the world. I was thoroughly impressed as he told the story of swimming with a great white shark! Well, safely in a cage, of course... but still, I was fascinated by this man. We laughed over each other's nightmare dating stories. At the end of the night, we shared a romantic kiss and decided to meet again for breakfast.

Just like old friends, we had another fun morning together before we each parted ways, with the promise to stay in touch. I felt as if I had met a prince. Though he considered himself a toad. Royalty with a touch of humility. I was smitten.

One day he asks me, "What are you up to next weekend?" "Oh nothing much" I say, trying to hide my hopeful enthusiasm.

"How would you like to go to the Salisbury Wine Fest?"

"I'd love to, send me a ticket!" Arrangements were made! Off I go for some jet-set dating!

I stepped off the plane, and there he is, waiting with that beautiful smile. I felt so comfortable, just like I saw him yesterday. We delivered a case of wine to his dear friends and then had a fun evening with his friends and family! I noted that he was actually introducing me to his inner circle! The wine fest the next day was cold but fun, and I actually helped him by selling the wine from his vineyard at his wine tent. OK, I'll work for wine, just keep my glass full! Afterwards, as we drove back, we spoke about expectations of partners in relationships. We were getting along so well. Then, just like that, he commented offhandedly, "I want to meet someone in my financial/educational bracket."

Had my Prince turned into a shallow Hal? I was crushed. How naive of me to think I was the only one he was dating. I was back where I started, humiliated and rejected. "Am I that pathetic?" I thought to myself.

I returned home very disappointed about the turn of circumstances. Weeks went by. He didn't call. Those old feelings of self-doubt begin to creep back in. "I'm not good enough. What's the matter with me? Who am I good enough for?" I started to second-guess my ability to choose a male companion. This belittling script played again and again in my head. Why was I giving into these feeling? Hadn't I

Thank God I...® Am an Empowered Woman:

learned that what others think of me doesn't change who I am?

My heart skipped a beat when the phone rang eight weeks later, and his name appeared on my caller I.D. I keep the conversation fun and light, mostly just catching up. Then we made plans to meet — but this time I knew it wasn't to be. He was still searching for his "equal," and I was no longer interested in waiting around. To learn to trust my heart again seemed futile on the one hand. On the other, it seemed the only way to move on. I was NOT going to be defeated. Good enough? Perhaps Mr. Vineyard wasn't "good enough" for me?

Dating Online is like playing a chess game. You stick to the rules about personal boundaries, you define what you want, and you keep your B.S. meter running. Months had passed since "The Big Kahuna," and I was now a savvy player. I knew that emotional, knee-jerk reaction that happens when someone pushes a button. I sniff out the hardcore Serial Daters.

I can sense the rejection and insecurities online. So many people yearning to be united. You can hear the need as you read their emails, "I thought I was the ONE!"... "You haven't written to me in 4 days, guess you have found something more interesting." This was my new social membership!

I sometimes waited days for a response. These are the times it feels as if your head and heart are going to collide. I have to constantly remind myself, "Enjoy the process. Don't take everything so seriously!"

After having spoken with so many people, after being rejected based on my finances, I truly learned so much about myself and other people. I realized that we all share so many fears, and deep inside, really what we are all searching for is to love ourselves and to be appreciated for who we are.

That's what I told myself when I got a wink from "Ace." We talked briefly, arranged to meet each other over lunch, and I spent two days trying not to be taken with anticipation and excitement. I was walking across the parking lot to the restaurant when I saw a man drive up in a sports car. "Could that be my date?" I thought. Then, quickly, I put that aside. "Could I be so shallow?" was what I thought next.

I quickly stepped into the restaurant, got seated, and waited with baited breath! A tall, mature, athletic man was walking towards me. Score! Is this the ONE? With nervous excitement we converse and are pleased with all we have in common. The interview was going well! Romantic, dog lover, traveler, intelligent, soft-spoken, mountain man! Thank you God! Hard to believe three years have gone by! We are planning for our future and still enjoying today!

The universe never fails to please me. I ask, and I shall receive! I don't ask why. I ask for clarification. I ask for the ability to view my patterns and results clearly. I ask for solutions and the ability to make change easily. If I don't get "it," I try again the next go around! I always remember it is all happening in God's time. With the courage to look within and get online I truly have changed my life. The process of my emotional evolution was quite the journey. I went through the anxiety of the unknown, the fear of self-discovery, and the pain of rejection; to find myself end up clear on the other side, with confidence, communication, and creation. I am a Creator. I am creating my life every day!

Thank God I... ® *Am an Empowered Woman:*

Do you believe in happy endings? Escaping into a romance novel showcasing strong heroines was a passion for me. The tantalizing romances and adventures started the journey of mind mapping for the perfect mate. This left me with a mission to become a woman of substance.

Entrepreneur, fun loving Christine, a health care provider, lives out her adventures in the mountains of Western North Carolina.

Contact her at: BellaDivasInc.com

Thank God I Have Muscular Dystrophy
By Heather Watkins

"For... the... rest... of... her... life," echoed in the empty hall of my mind. I read the words over and over from the doctor's diagnosis letter for disability and then looked away. My heart beat fast, my hands became clammy, and the lump in my throat grew with every shallow breath. "Ya know you will have to consider a lifestyle change and slow things down significantly," the doctor stated. My face hardened and contorted as if he was speaking ancient Greek. "If I slow things down any further, I'll be standing still," was my response to the doctor. Born with Muscular Dystrophy, a degenerative muscle disease, and although ambulatory, I was used to moving at a physically slower pace and was living relatively normally... until now. Things were about to change.

"You have become hypoxic due to the weakening of your diaphragmatic muscle which aids your lungs when breathing. It is causing you to retain more carbon dioxide and less oxygen when you sleep. That is why you have trouble sleeping and migraines when you wake up," the doctor

explained. I was exhausted during the day so much so that my chest ached and my hands trembled. Barely able to keep concentration, I was nodding off in meetings at work. Even worse, and although it was a short drive to get there, I was drowsy while driving on the highway! Saddest of all was my daughter getting a part-time mother who was becoming less sensitive to her needs.

Thank God I... ® *Am an Empowered Woman:*

"You will need to have oxygen therapy at home which will be given through a ventilator nightly and whenever you nap. This device will assist you in breathing," he further explained. Is he kidding? I am not old, and wearing a breathing mask is NOT my idea of sexy! Isn't there some other alternative? What does he mean I should stop working? What will I do in the meantime? How will I be able to properly provide for my daughter and myself? Will my insurance cover this? The questions assembled around me like after school bullies waiting for an answer to a schoolyard challenge! And yet, I had no reply; instead, I held my breath, clutching pretend pearls.

I returned home and sank into the couch sullen, weary, with a partial plan, and pondered my predicament. I gave myself permission to pout and feel sorry; somehow it felt satisfying while I waited for my daughter to return from school. What else was I going to lose? I sighed, rolled my eyes and threw my hands up in frustration. No longer did I have the ability to spring forth from a chair, run down the stairs or pick up things dropped on the floor. I've cried inside so many times about not being able to fluidly sway my hips fearing I might fall, thus ignoring the tempting invitation of a radios blaring beat. I could now feel the fluctuations of the ground, and it was harder to adjust. I reluctantly began ambulating with a cane five years ago. My vanity took a hit but a steady, stabilized gait spelled safety.

What would my daughter think of me? How would she view her mother now? What kind of mother am I capable of being? I was counting my cant's and they were piled high, yet I was strangely comforted by the quiet. There was a joy in being alone with my thoughts, a joy in having time to think.

I thought about how I enjoyed being a mother, how I enjoyed being *her* mother. I didn't have a clear vision of how motherhood would be with a disability or how it would change me and the *way* I mothered. Yet here I was, and she was growing up. I could continue to feel sorry for myself and let time pass, or I could decide to be the best version of myself... from this day forward. And be at peace with that. Ultimately, my daughter would get her cues from that example and decide who she would become. This, I realized, was vitally important!

As my thoughts gravitated towards my daughter, I thought back to a time when she was much smaller and her health and physical safety were a higher priority. A mother is always concerned with her child's health and safety, but being a mother with a disability made me hyper-concerned. I remember when we'd leave the house, I'd put a "death grip" on her little wrist so she wouldn't wriggle free and run away from me as I didn't have the ability to run after her.

I feared she would wander into the street with oncoming traffic or fall, and I'd be unable to pick her up. It was a gripping terror, I felt so incomplete as a person and mother. I did my best to provide a safe, nurturing environment, and where I lacked in physical ability, I made a concerted effort in an emotional connection — singing, reading, hugging, and teaching. As we'd often sit in quiet, I learned the beauty of being in the best place to intercept the best thoughts — stillness.

Yet, here I was again with another reminder of why I wasn't complete — progression of my disability. "You aren't good enough. You aren't like the other mothers. You can't keep up, things will only get worse," the debilitating thoughts were hitting me like a battering ram, crushing my ego and self-worth. "You are not your body and so what if you're not like other able-bodied mothers. You are unique because you are YOU," said a small voice inside that seemed to wade through and rise above the muck.

My feelings were indicative of my thoughts, so I chose to pay attention to them and became aware of where my thinking needed to be adjusted or amplified. I may not have had control over being born with a disability but I certainly had control over my thoughts about it. I could choose my internal dialogue. I could choose the thoughts I was feeding myself. This realization was empowering, and I felt the fogginess lifting, and a slight smile slid across my face. Suddenly the room didn't feel so small, nor the world too big to navigate.

Maybe I wasn't a mom who could run, jump, and bond with her child playing sports, but I could certainly strengthen our bond by keeping the lines of communication open, giving her age appropriate awareness about what it means to be living in the world and how we are all connected. This shift felt magical, as if I was awakening from some slumber. I had been "sleepwalking," and living had become so routine. I didn't even remember her favorite color; the small details that mattered were fading into oblivion.

It has taken me years and effort to feel comfortable in my skin. It's a process of peeling back layers of the past as well as stopping "old tapes" playing in my head that were on a continuous loop. Perhaps evolution, age, and grace play a factor in revealing new skin, working internally much the same way dermabrasion does effacing blemishes and marks externally. My nocturnal breathing has stabilized, and I enjoy a night's sleep rested and no longer waking up with migraines and nausea from too much carbon dioxide buildup in the blood thanks to mechanical ventilation. Being alive and alert is the new sexy!

The keys turned in the lock and my daughter's brown eyes met mine as she came through the door. "Hey Mom, I have something I want you to read," handing over an essay from her College Prep class she'd written as she's now seventeen and navigating the college process. The assignment was to write about a person whose impact has been significant, and to my sheer delight the subject was me!

My eyes feasted on lines that described how I'd shaped her worldview and self-image. My heart swelled and spirit danced, whirling like the Dervish, with the sentence: "I never was embarrassed because Muscular Dystrophy is what made her special to me." Imparting wisdom she learned: "Over the years I have learned from her how to reach out to others, how to stay strong through adversity, and how to be happy and satisfied with the present time." And lastly, her deep gratitude for lessons learned: "I enjoy the present time and I live for this moment I am in right now. I have a big heart and I am a fighter in whatever I do. Thanks Mom."

I hugged my daughter and embraced the ever-evolving me. I kissed her on the forehead, drew in a breath and... exhaled.

Heather Watkins is a disability advocate, graduate of Emerson College with a degree in Mass Communications and a lifelong resident of Boston, Massachusetts. She is a mother of a teen daughter, loves reading, daydreaming, and chocolate. Heather also enjoys listening to music, writing "thank you" notes, and promoting goodwill. She is currently involved in a community project to increase accessibility to local businesses for people with disabilities.

Thank God the Plane Crashed
By Nikki Vescovi

Wow, there he was looking at me. His deep brown eyes seemed to magnetically be drawn to mine as he looked across the room. The room was pumping with music and my heart was pounding. I could feel it jump to my throat as he approached me. There was a cheeky smile on his face as he turned to me and said, "Wanna dance?" and presumptively grabbed my hand. I suddenly found myself pulled onto the dance floor into a throng of sweating bodies.

The Beta house was known for "the wild and crazy" nature of its members, and this night was no exception. Meatloaf's "Paradise by the Dashboard Light" began to play, and I found myself caught up in the song as the girls challenged their partners, screaming, "I've got to know right now, before we go any further, do you love me? Will you love me forever?" While the guys pushed back saying, "Let me sleep on it... baby, baby, let me sleep on it. I'll give you my answer in the morning."

The intensity between me and my partner just seemed to grow and that little voice inside my head said, "Uh, ohh... you're in trouble." I just had the feeling this one was a "bad" boy, but there was no resisting it. I was the moth to the flame.

Ironically, "Paradise by the Dashboard Light" seemed a perfect theme. It's amazing the crazy things you do when you are consumed by passion. It was all so exciting and exhilarating. Probably, I knew somewhere in the back of mind that anything that burned so brightly would have an equally tragic demise and would crash in flames. Even though the relationship only lasted a few months, I still was stubbornly determined to make it work and when the kickoff party for the big Beta event — the Beta 500 — came, after the breakup, I saw my opportunity.

The crowd was packed tightly into an outdoor enclosure. I must have been crazy thinking this would be my opportunity. There were so many people and way too many hot girls everywhere. I wouldn't stand a chance. And then, there he was. His eyes caught mine, but this time he just looked right through me, like I didn't even exist. Don't pretend not to see me, you jerk! I know you can. I pushed my way forward, toward him, and I could feel the vibe already... . He seemed to act like he'd never seen me before. "Well," I thought, "you sure knew me when I didn't have my clothes on." I was angry, hurt and just plain pissed off as I approached him, but I was determined to maintain my dignity. "Hey, how are you?" I thought it sounded pretty nonchalant, though even in my own head, I could hear the voice sounded pinched and just a little bitchy.

The blonde that was hanging all over him gave me a total look of disgust as if I was a bug beneath her foot. She looked icily pristine, and I knew I didn't stand a chance. I withered under her glance, and I clearly got the message, "Stay off my turf." He turned to me and the look was totally devoid of feeling. That one look told me all I needed to know, and I felt a deep pain in my heart. "How could you, after everything?" I thought to myself. Whatever paradise there had once been now turned to a hell in my own mind, and I just wanted to get out... get out of this throng of people as fast as I could.

Thank God it was a college campus on a Friday night. There was always a party somewhere, so I headed over to another pre-Beta celebration event. I knew I wanted just one thing to obliterate him out of my mind and to forget that look of total disdain that had left me feeling less than nothing. Somehow I managed to find my way home, peel off my clothes, and crawl into bed.

I groggily awoke to my sister shaking me. "I'm leaving now... for the Beta. See you later," she said. Her message barely registered as I fell back into the depths of my drunken depression and the darkness descended on me. I found myself wandering in a dream in a dark cold room where I was completely alone and panicking desperately.

Suddenly, the room was shaking. "Am I still in the dream?" I thought, but the shaking continued, rocking me awake. Okay, so it's not the dream. The room is definitely shaking. In my dazed, semi-hungover state, my mind couldn't find the logic as this was Bowling Green, Ohio, not Los Angeles, California. The room kept shaking and my mind continued to search for an answer... perhaps this was World War III? Again, not exactly likely that it would begin in a small college town in northwest Ohio! Thank God the shaking finally ended. Thanks to all the activities of the night before, I fell back asleep. It just must be a part of my crazy dream.

Seconds later there was a huge explosion which was impossible to sleep through. Again, my mind searched for an answer. Was it a bomb? After all, I had grown up in England in the 1970s and had gotten used to the ideas of bombs exploding in unexpected moments. No, perhaps it was that my sister had somehow managed to blow the furnace. Whatever it was, it was too hard to ignore this time, so I jumped out of bed and went to the door leading to the front room.

Opening the door was like opening the front of an incredibly hot oven. It was like an inferno. The moment I opened the door the heat smacked me in the face. Luckily, I am incredibly nearsighted, so I couldn't make out much. All I could see was that the room was engulfed in flames. I heard my other roommate, Jody, screaming, "Get out of here... get out of here." I threw my long, royal blue, velvet robe over my naked body and ran out the back door. It always amazes me how our natural survival instincts take over in moments such as this. I didn't give one thought to what I should take from the room, I ran out in my blue, velour robe and didn't even grab my contact lenses, which I desperately needed to see.

Thank God there is a front and back door to the apartment, so I can get out of here. At that moment, everything in my room was intact, and I had no idea that I would never see ANY of my possessions ever again.

I walked out the back door, moving away from the apartment, to discover a very surreal sight. Heavy, thick smoke was pouring from the top of our apartment at least 50 to 100 feet in the air. What could have happened? I felt completely dazed and confused. I was totally disheveled and couldn't make out much of anything as I had left my contact lenses in the apartment. As a group of evacuees from the apartment gathered on the side of the road away from the heat, flames, and smoke, the news began to spread.

Apparently, a Piper Cherokee plane had taken off from the county airport, which bordered the apartment complex on the edge of the college campus. The pilot had miscalculated the weight ratio and had taken on another passenger at the airport, which proved to be one too many. The plane had taken off from the airport and had been unable to takeoff correctly, literally crashing into our front room (while I lay practically unconscious in the bedroom). All four of the college-aged students in the plane burned to death in my front room.

Luckily, no one in the apartment building I lived in was hurt. However, everything we owned was gone. As my sister and I went back to the burned remains of our apartment all that was left was ashes... ashes of our former lives never to be recovered. For me, this meant everything from college PLUS everything I brought with me high school in England was gone. It felt like my life had been wiped out in one fell swoop.

So imagine this... imagine you are leaving your home as you do every day. You leave your home or apartment, and everything is fine. That night, you come home to find that everything you owned is gone and all that is left is ashes. Imagine the feeling of loss and devastation that would sweep over you knowing you will NEVER see any of it again.

For me, this had additional consequences. I was in the fourth year of what was turning out to be a five-year program. I had one more year left to complete my Bachelor of Science degree in marketing and desperately wanted to go into advertising. My dreams went up in smoke as I had lost everything that was in my advertising portfolio: all my drawings, photographs, clippings, and all the work done in my advertising, graphics, and design classes. Long before digital renderings, thousands of hours of work, all original, were lost forever and would be impossible to replicate. I felt completely crushed.

On top of that, I now felt responsible for myself and my younger sister as we had both been living in the apartment. My parents still lived in England. Imagine the call to my parents, "Hey, mom and dad, how are you?... Yeah, we are fine... A plane just landed in our front room!" We had no clothes, all of our books and notes for classes were gone, and we had nowhere to live.

Worst of all, I would try to go to sleep and every sound would wake me up, reminding me of the event. Dreams were consumed with the feeling of being back in the shaking room with the flames raging at the bedroom door. It was next to impossible to focus and concentrate on any studies, and we became "minor" celebrities on campus which, in itself, became even more distracting and confusing. How were we to rebuild our lives? Where would my career go? How would I ever pull the pieces together for me and my sister? It had all crashed just as it had at the moment when I saw the blonde with my ex-boyfriend.

Yet, in the moment of my greatest challenge I saw my greatest opportunity. It was as if people came from nowhere to assist me. As I stood beside the blazing apartment, someone took pity on my bedraggled form and offered to let me come into their apartment. They kindly just gave me sweatpants and a t-shirt so I at least, had something to wear. To this day I don't know who that was or where they came from, but the support just seemed to magically appear.

Once I had the clothes, I walked toward my sorority house as I knew everyone would be there because of the Beta 500. Luckily, my best friend, Liz, had an extra pair of contact lenses which I could see through, and I wore those. The university gave us dorm rooms to stay in for the rest of the year, and our professors were more than understanding given the situation. The Red Cross helped with clothing. People I never met on campus and in the local community donated items to us to help us get through. It really reminded me of the absolute goodness in people. I saw how we are truly connected, even on the unseen level.

Thank God I... ® *Am an Empowered Woman:*

There had been that moment of total desolation, despair, and yet in the moment of losing everything, I gained everything. I gained a new freedom, independent of my possessions and what I had been in the past. I realized that though I had felt isolated and alone, a moment such as this created an awareness of a much deeper and everlasting connection.

Thanks to this event I have been inspired to focus on *The Power of Connection,* knowing that at the end of the day things are replaceable, people are not. After all, my sister should have been dead in the front room. That was where she would have been on a Saturday morning, smoking a cigarette and drinking her cup of coffee. This day she had been spared.

Because I had lost my advertising portfolio, I turned my marketing degree toward sales. I have now been in the sales profession for 30 years. This has been the best thing that ever happened to me, and I now teach others how to sell. The word "sales" comes from a root word which means "to serve." I am so grateful for getting this opportunity thanks to the cash.

This has taught me that no matter what happens to me, it will work out. I have lost everything once and come through okay, so the fear of losing it again is not so great. As humans, I know we have an incredible ability to pull through, especially in what appears to be our darkest hour.

I know this because, besides the plane crash, my entire family was run down by a drun-driver in Germany when I was 10-years old...and in 1991 I was rescued by the Jaws of Life when a truck drove over my car!

Besides mastering these traumatic events, I also discovered that external "things" do not validate me. No boyfriend, job, partner, or possession ever defined who I truly am, for I am always so much more. And I see through new eyes how much I have to be grateful for.

So, I thank God for the plane crash. This event has truly defined my life, helped me see the incredible gifts we all are given, and let me say thank you for the opportunity to celebrate every moment of every day... we truly never know when it will be our last.

Master of *The Power of Connection*, Nikki Vescovi knows what it feels like to be an outsider. She is a sought out communication expert, coaching leaders in four continents around the world, delivering a 600% sales increase for one client. She demystifies how to influence others and gain an even deeper understanding of oneself.

Thank God I Found Acceptance
By Teresa McDowell

I relived that dream over and over again... the one where you spend your entire sleeping hours looking for something but can't find it. Drifting back and forth in-between dream state and awake, the search continued. I pursued my purpose in life, my spiritual identity, and the meaning of my existence. This quest consumed me and placed me in a box. I felt like I needed to have a label for everything and define my every move. The tornado of control whipped me around, attempting to knock some sense into me, but I incessantly sought fulfillment anywhere I could locate it.

I reached my breaking point in 2003. It was like plunging head first into an open pool with no water. My business started sinking, the debt started rising, and my husband struggled daily with Ross River Virus. I was 37 with three small children living in outback Kalgoorlie, Western Australia wondering how to avoid a dead end. Every morning at 4:30 AM, he rode to work on his push bike, with the rain crashing down on him, exhausted from fighting the joint disease. It hurt to see him so worn down, and then my work schedule kept me away from my family, especially during the early years, which crushed me. I needed and wanted to be there for them more than anything. Difficult choices lay ahead of me; that's when the fear sank in.

In the many long, lonely hours in my store, as the business was sinking & struggling to make ends meet, I sat and dreamt of ways that I could not only get myself and my family out of this situation, but also make a real difference in the world. That's when it hit me. I could profile Industrial Hemp. I had always felt passionate about Hemp and its benefits for as long as I could remember. It seemed to me that this misunderstood resource could impact both the environment and personal wellbeing in such a positive way. Why wouldn't the world embrace it? This was my chance to turn things around.

We closed the business, cut our losses, and headed back to my home state of South Australia. With NO work on the horizon, NO home to live in, and the guilt of my business debt over my head, we packed up all our belongings and headed into the unknown. I remember driving across the vast platform of limestone, also known as the Nullarbor Plain, feeling such great peace; the rainbow that cast itself across the endless desert, also called The Road Sign of the Gods, gave me faith that our life was about to change for the better. I leaned towards the open window, and let the wind tousle my hair and tickle my heart. Certainty washed over me, and I concluded that my passion for hemp and the hemp industry was a path I needed to pursue. For the first time in a long time, I was excited!

The coming weeks were incredibly breathtaking. Events, people, and places all seemed to conspire to help us. Everything just fell into place with little effort. I still look back on this time with great wonder as it was a time of complete manifestation, evolving from a place of nothingness when all you have are possibilities. Within one week of arriving in Adelaide, we had happily settled in a community of like-minded people, enrolled our three children at the Mount Barker Waldorf School, and had found a lovely home to rent close by.

Simon was miraculously recovering and feeling stronger every day. He managed to land a great job which included international travel and a company car, and I was now finally free to start working from home on my vision for

Thank God I... ® Am an Empowered Woman:

Hemp Hemp Hooray. Thank God the balance in my life had returned! The vision for my business was clear, and I had formulated the products; all I needed now was capital. I first wrote a nine page business plan with financial projections for the future, and then naively and somewhat arrogantly, approached our local bank for funding to get this dream off the ground. I truly believed I would persuade them, and it worked! Regardless of us lacking a decent financial position and having no personal assets, they believed in my vision enough and offered me a micro loan to kick things off.

Alright, the ball was rolling. The momentum energized me. SCREECH! BOOM! Another roadblock?! Just as I was beginning to feel like my life was taking a turn for the better, I received frustrating news. Our conservative establishments resisted the promoting and selling of Industrial Hemp for they wrongly associated it with its cousin marijuana. I had problems even registering my business name for they believed it was promoting the illicit drug element. I felt myself deflating like a balloon, and then I began to frantically contemplate a solution.

What to do? Well... fast forward two years, and I was still working from home formulating my products in my kitchen and balancing my children's needs while my husband regularly worked away. Cash flow was becoming a major problem, and we were faced with the possibility of taking our children out of their unique, rich learning environment as we could no longer afford the school fees. Something had to give, so I took a second job at a men's clothing store to pay for their education. It would be a while before I was out of the red, and we still had debts from the previous business.

My mission and aspirations carried me through the next 18 months. I figured if I couldn't do the hemp business purely for the love of it then what was the point. Therefore, I continued to build the foundation. I worked part-time and saw to the needs of three children while Simon was travelling all over the country. The icy, cold seawater enveloped me and my body continued to fall to the ocean floor. No air, no light, just darkness. Would this business decision take me back to the same emotional place I was in from the shop in Kalgoorlie? Struggling to make ends meet again and no time for my family, I wondered if I was searching once again in vain.

You might as well have told me that I was Dorothy from The Wizard of Oz and that I was in her Kansas home trying to survive the tornado. The depression had started to set in at this point; the anger, exhaustion, and frustration followed thereafter. If my soul were a mood ring, the color would have never changed from black. A happy face out in public was doable, but behind closed doors, things were dreadful. I never realized at the time how much my condition affected my husband. Like most men, all he wanted to do was fix everything, but not being able to do so tore him up inside. He somehow endured the pain and stood by me, as did my children. I don't even want to think how I affected them.

I had read many inspirational and spiritual books in the past, but I couldn't seem to put into practice any of the techniques to pull myself up from this destructive place. So many nights the tears streamed down my face like a faucet kept on for hours. The sadness shifted to guilt as I'd lie there thinking about how I should feel grateful as opposed to dissatisfied. I felt exhausted and trapped having to work two jobs and had lost all my passion for my business. I was only going through the motions, so the business began to crumble, along with my spirit.

That's when I purchased a book by Eckhart Tolle, A New Earth, which I read almost reluctantly at first. It was making a lot of sense to me, but still I felt indifferent and then — Oh My God! There it was; the fog disappeared, making the path ever so visible to my weepy eyes. The answer to rekindling my flame lay right in the final chapters. A simple prescription to follow — it said something to this affect: In order for you to have peace in your life there should be at least one of three elements (if not all three) running through your life.

Enthusiasm... Enjoyment... Acceptance.

I had NO Enthusiasm for my business, job or life, and I felt NO Enjoyment for these things either, but I could ACCEPT my situation. I had an emotional release, except this time it was tears of hope not tears of despair. I cried long and hard, cleansing my soul of its burdens. YES, I could move forward and end this cycle of despair. In my mind, I drifted back to that day when we drove across the never-ending flatlands, where Heaven meets Earth in such a majestic way that it takes your breath away, and I knew it with absolute certainly now. I was home.

Yes, I still face many challenges as the business continues to grow; however, I am still prepared to extend myself and take risks, keeping the dream moving forward. I have now moved the business out of my kitchen and into our fabulous new production warehouse (that my talented husband built) with exports to the US and customers connecting with us from all over the globe through our online store. I have learned that we always have a choice in every situation and if we can maintain belief in the uniqueness of ourselves and harness the strength of our infinite potential then there is nothing we cannot achieve. I am no longer searching, there is meaning in every moment, I have found my purpose in life, and my spirituality is LOVE.

♥♥♥

Teresa McDowell is the wife of an incredible husband, mother to three amazing children, and founder of Hemp Hemp Hooray Natural Body Care — organic hemp skin care that heals and rejuvenates with love. It is her hope that other women facing similar difficulties in balancing the challenges of being a businesswoman, wife, and mother can find inspiration to continue in the pursuit of their own passions and dreams. Teresa can be reached through her website HempHempHooray.com.au

Thank God I Found Faith
By Faith Deeter

I was born premature but healthy, and my parents named me Faith. My growing up was basically normal, and then at the age of twenty, I was diagnosed with Hodgkin's Lymphoma cancer. The cancer came with a single message: Be real, be on the outside who I truly am on the inside.

That's why I pulled off my shoes before sliding over the glossy, smooth back of the white stallion. It just seemed like the real thing to do.

The white prom dress I was wearing was arranged in huge ruffles around me. I moved my horse into the surf and galloped bareback over the wet sand while salt water sprayed and his hooves splashed and pounded. My mother took photos. The next day, week six of chemo, I would cut off my hair and keep it. Rather than lose my hair, I would cut it and store it in a box in the closet. But today, I would not think of any of these things. In this moment, gliding along the shoreline in the sun, I was happy.

It was a time in my life when things were crystal clear, and for a short time, I knew the meaning of my life. I knew what mattered to me, and I knew what didn't. I knew my capabilities, and I knew my limitations. I knew exactly what I wanted to do and nothing could stop me from doing it. No risk was too great. No embarrassment too daunting. No cost too high. In fact, there was no cost in doing things; there was only cost in not doing them. My entire perspective on life changed instantly, and I found a new alignment.

The alarm of imminent death became a great gift for propulsion for living. It seemed like no accident that just two weeks prior I had read the book *Illusions*, by Richard Bach, and learned that what I had believed were limits were not limits at all. When compared to death itself, fears I had allowed to control me vanished. What others thought of me was no longer relevant. I dared to do things I never would have done before because all of the sudden time mattered. Time mattered, other people mattered, and for the first time in my life, I understood just how much I mattered.

But why I mattered was the surprising thing. Bald and waif-like, I was no longer beautiful. Weak and weary, I was no longer athletic. Drugged and bedraggled, my memory was so impaired it felt like a dream that I had ever been smart. Compared with what I had been able to achieve just a few months prior, I was essentially useless, so why I mattered turned out to be a simple and pleasant surprise.

I mattered because I was alive and for no other reason than I was me and alive. I was the only Faith that would ever live and the only one that could fulfill the unique potential of my life. When I was young, my piano teacher referred to me often as her 'unlimited potential gal,' and ill, weak, and weary though I was, I finally understood the potential innately available within me — potential I did not have to earn and potential that would never go away despite my circumstances. A simple and profound gift came in knowing that my primary purpose in life was to simply be Faith, and to truly be Faith, what I had to do was be real; be on the outside who I was on the inside, and the rest would simply unfold.

Being real, however, did not always make other people comfortable. Still in college, I registered for classes, and too weak to stand, I sat in line and scooted forward. Others looked on with uneasy glances, but that didn't bother me.

I took a simple class, The Psychology of Women, and when I refused to go along with the teacher's position that all women are victims, my journal came back with the following comment, "You are dangerous."

The label stung. A friend of mine cautioned me, "When one person's thinking gets too far from other people's thinking, no one can relate to them anymore." "Great," I thought. "So what you're telling me is that unless I change, I will be alone." It wasn't that I was trying to change or not trying to change. All I was trying to do was live my life, and I had nothing to lose except body parts. That is truly how I looked at things at the time — nothing to lose but body parts and everything to gain.

Then, I almost lost my life. I had a bad reaction to the chemo drugs and my intestines shut down. In excruciating pain, the doctor assumed I was constipated and gave me a jug of liquid called "Go Lightly," which I drank as quickly as I could. The problem was I wasn't constipated, so when they gave me a second gallon, my poor intestines stretched even further. I can't say how I knew, but I just knew that within hours, my intestines would rupture, and I would die.

Neither my mother nor I could get the nurses to understand. When the pain got so intense that I could no longer withhold crying, the tears only seemed to make it more difficult for the nurses to get it. "They think I'm overreacting," I realized, "and I'm supposed to sit here and be a good patient while they let me die."

My mother knew me; she believed me. "Call Stanford," I told her. "Tell them my colon is going to rupture and I will die." I'd seen specialists at Stanford University Hospital, so my mother dialed them. The answering service took her message. Several minutes passed. No call back. "Call again," I said. "You have to keep calling." She called again, then again, and again.

The doctor that my mother finally reached around 2 a.m. yelled at her for her persistence, but he heard what she was saying and within minutes I had an x-ray, a surgeon, tubes shoved in various places to vacuum away pressure, and thankfully, finally, morphine. My mother's and my own persistence saved my life. If not for that, I would not be here.

It was an important lesson in being willing to act in accordance with myself even when the experts were telling me I was wrong. It was an important lesson in being willing to upset other people, disregard authority, and reject protocol. When your guts are screaming: "You're gonna die," it pays to listen to your guts.

Too often in the past, I had refused to act because acting in accordance with my gut instinct was unfamiliar and not always well received. I'd been raised by good parents to be a good person and obey life's rules, but I was finally learning, as was my mother, there is a time and a place to say, "No."

When my intestines finally stabilized, my white cell count plunged to zero, and I spiked a fever. "This is finally it," I thought. "Just don't let me die alone." That's when I heard the voice. It said, "We are born alone. We die alone. We can spend our time with others, but ultimately, we are alone."

I'd heard the voice before. The first time I heard it, I was walking to the barn to feed my horse and was wondering what more I could lose and still be alive. It wasn't an act of feeling sorry for myself; it was more an act of accounting.

I imagined myself as a large ball and every time I identified something that was no longer a part of me, a piece of the ball detached and went away. I had lost my hair, my looks, my stamina, and strength. I could no longer ride my bike or my horse and had stopped trying. My memory was gone. As one piece after another disappeared, the ball became smaller and smaller. Finally, what had been a sizeable ball was reduced to a small black dot. That small black dot was what remained of me.

What was this tiny speck? Who was I if I was no longer the capable woman I'd believed myself to be? In my mind's eye, I zoomed in for a closer look, and the tiny black speck became a key hole. I was drawn to look inside the keyhole. I heard a whoosh, and the other side opened up to become a vast, starry, universal sky. It was stunningly silent, peaceful, and beautiful. In that moment, I heard the voice from deep within me say, "You can never lose your Self."

I'm not sure if I was shocked, awed, or stupefied. What did it mean? When all the things I'd thought were me dropped away, I was the universe? Could I be making this up or could it be some strange reaction to the chemo drugs?

If it were true, I was not less than I'd thought myself to be, I was more. I was vast, graceful, gently powerful, and as limitless as the universe. If it were true for me, it would be true for all of us. In that moment I realized that at our core, all of us are sacred.

Cancer taught me many things, but most importantly, it brought me to my Self. The message was simple, "Be real. Be who you are. Limits are illusions. You are powerful beyond measure. What other people think of you does not matter. What you think of yourself does. You may feel alone at times, but there is a wisdom that will guide you if you let it. You can utilize yourself and your life."

I know now, we are each powerful and special beyond measure. At our core, each one of us is sacred, and everybody matters.

Faith Deeter, MFT, is a licensed therapist, author, speaker, and certified trainer. In 2003, she founded Galloping Thru Life therapeutic riding program. Today, Faith teaches relationship courses at a federal prison, has lectured at Johns Hopkins University, and offers personal development training. She is the author of *The Conflict Pattern Revealed* and *Live Alligned With The Real You*. Her work has been featured on numerous radio shows and in print publications.

Thank God I Spent Time With My Mother
By Inez Bracy

Being the sixth child of seven I watched as my older siblings left home and their chores fell to the next oldest. I watched in horror as it became my turn; my turn for tending the summer garden, cooking and cleaning the house. My mom always prided herself on having a beautiful flower garden (taken care of by the children). My turn saw the flowers overgrown with weeds, and the garden in total disrepair... .

I can still hear our laughter blending with the breeze that flows through the palm trees of South Florida. In order to escape the rough winters of Virginia, my mom would travel down South and stay with me for a couple of months starting in January. She loved visiting because it gave her a certain status among her friends. She was the only one who "wintered in Florida" every year!

Those winters we spent together were a highlight in my life. Even though her social calendar was full, she'd still make time for me! My mom was open to new adventures and didn't judge, like most people do. On those days that we spent together, we did all kinds of things, from shopping in Palm Beach, to actually attending a real Sweat Lodge Ceremony! She was truly one of a kind and always came from a place of love. Perhaps that is the reason so many people loved her.

After a few years, a position in Ohio popped up that I simply couldn't turn down; however, the environment took a little getting used to. I definitely loved my work and started to enjoy the winters, but whenever I'd talk with my mom she'd say, "I really miss Florida." The longing in her voice tugged at my heartstrings. I desperately missed our special time together and didn't want to give it up. So I decided that the first chance I got I'd move back to Florida.

Within six months, I was offered a position in Central Florida that utilized my skills and talents, so I snatched it right up. When I called my mom to tell her the news, I could feel her beaming through the phone, and I could taste her excitement. All was right with the world!

While I was unpacking my belongings and sorting through the mess, I received word of her diagnosis. Just when I thought my life was back in order, the carpet was pulled out from underneath me. However, I refused to believe that her cancer would impact our plans, because I just knew she would be healed.

During that first year, my mom was able to live independently, but her treatments hindered her from traveling south for the winter. She just needed more time to heal. Next year, we would be celebrating her recovery and sipping on iced tea under the sun. She just needed a little more time.

But her poor body began to weaken so quickly. She couldn't live on her own anymore, so she moved in with my sister in North Carolina.

Then, the year of the hurricanes happened, one right behind the other. I would be glued to the Weather Channel. Whenever the hurricane track looked like it would possibly hit Florida, I'd rush off to North Carolina. Nothing stopped me from visiting her, laughing with her, and holding her hand. I flew up there at least four times that year, spending a week or more with her and my sis each time. I remained hopeful, but with each trip, her body became more and more frail.

Thank God I... ® *Am an Empowered Woman:*

When I walked into my sister's home for the last hurricane, my mom stopped in the middle of what she was doing, looked up with surprise and said, "Do you still have a job?" Laughingly I said, "Yes, a hurricane is on the way." On this trip, my mom made sure I left on time for my return to Florida.

The next day my sister took my mom for her treatments. When the phone rang in my office, I didn't want to answer it. My heart was beating so fast, but I lifted the phone off of the receiver and placed it next to my ear. "Mom has been hospitalized and it doesn't look good." My sister's voice was so shaky and broken. My brother called immediately after to tell me, "Don't worry; you know how Esther gets upset easily." I decided to disregard my brother's advice and made my reservation for the next day. I do not recall any of the drive to the airport. I remember landing and getting into a taxi to go to the hospital.

I wanted to check into the hotel across the street but my sister didn't want me to leave her. So I slept on a recliner, with my suitcase at my feet, in the room provided for family of terminal patients. (I wasn't aware of this at the time). The doctor came and got me at 2 am because my mom was awake. "I can't believe you're here and that I'm lying here in this hospital!" We laughed about that.

By 10 a.m. all of the family had arrived except one (the one with Power of Attorney). She had gone to a conference and was having difficulty getting a flight. We all consulted with the doctors as we could see that mom was failing fast. She was now on life support, which she never wanted. The doctors had a new procedure they wanted to try that would give her an iffy 30% chance to live.

When my sister arrived, she and I went into my mom's room. My mom was just lying with tubes in her nose and throat but could hear us. My sister asked her, "Squeeze my hand if you hear me." And she did. My sister then asked, "Squeeze my hand if you want these tubes removed." She asked three times and my mom squeezed her hand three times. The tubes were removed and all of the family gathered around her bed singing as she made her transition.

My dear mother's spirit floated away with the wind on September 30, 2004.

Nothing made sense anymore. My work didn't even interest me. My anticipated duties had changed and without our visits to look forward to, I wanted everything to disintegrate. A lust for life and contentment vanished, along with our talks, our giggles, and our hugs.

I needed her. I needed her guidance and her encouragement. Her memory wasn't good enough. "Mom, what am I going to do? What do you think I should do?" No response. As the days rolled into weeks, and the weeks into months, the hurricane inside of me began to blow gale force winds, and I realized very clearly that my reasons for being there were no longer valid. I'd taken the job because I wanted to have a place for my mom to visit in the winter. I'd taken the job because it offered me the opportunity to grow and use my skills. Without that I had nothing.

Of course I ignored the signs and plunged on ahead. I simply wore a mask to cover up my bleeding heart. My perfectly constructed façade helped me to wear a smile at work and act friendly as to not entice my coworkers to hound me with questions.

Thank God I... ® *Am an Empowered Woman:*

Even a family vacation to Jamaica didn't help. I was able to relax for about two seconds, but as soon as we returned home, I became very ill. I was already battling my thoughts, but now I had to battle the physical symptoms that were pleading with me to pay attention. The tears and the pain gushed out of me as if someone had obliterated the walls of a dam.

I was terrified of the future and of making an impulsive decision, but if I walked into that office one more time, I knew I would die. That's when I heard her. "It's going to be alright, baby." My mom always did know how to comfort me with her soft and tender spirit. That's when I realized that the only way to quiet the storm was to resign from my job, so I did.

My lungs expanded, and I could actually breathe again. Blood flowed through my veins once more, all the way to my fingertips, and my dying spirit awakened after a long period of numbness. But now what? Mom! Oh mom! I need your help again!

I took a look at my options and at my skill set, and I made up my mind to start my own business. I had some money saved and knew that I could live off of it for two years. Who knew what would happen after that. My body was trembling with fear and excitement all at the same time.

She was no longer here to calm me down and experience the highs and lows with me. But I knew she wanted me to be happy. My mom had always encouraged us to live our dreams. "Nothing beats a failure but a try!" Somehow this always made me feel better, and I'd continue on.

I quit my job when it changed so significantly that I became physically ill. Five years later, I am an award winning author, coach, speaker, and radio and TV personality. I love

Awakening Your Inner Strength and Genius...

helping women rediscover, rejuvenate and redefine their lives. I live in gratitude and appreciation daily.

Inez is a masterful coach, engaging keynote speaker, trainer, and seminar presenter. She provides clarity, excitement, and momentum infused with confidence.

Thank God I Am a Breast Cancer Survivor and Thriver
By Nilla Spark

I walked into the doctor's room, and I knew without words being spoken... then I heard what I didn't want to hear. "Nilla, I'm sorry... ." I finished her sentence by saying, "I have breast cancer, don't I?" The doctor looked at me and nodded. I fell sobbing into John's arms, thinking, "I am going to die." We hugged each other for what felt like forever; all my fears and emotions around dying surfaced. Would I die like my mother had? What will happen to John? I didn't want him to become a widower! Who would look after our business, our home? What is ahead of us? My mind spun out of control!

This wasn't meant to happen. Even though the odds were stacked against me, I told myself that cancer wouldn't occur in my life. My doctor, on one of my normal checkups, told me to be diligent with my breast examinations, as my chances of getting breast cancer were very high. She said that my mother having passed away due to breast cancer and my Nonna having had both breasts removed were huge contributors. Also, I had undergone five IVF treatments, and had not had children, subsequently had not breast fed... BLAH BLAH BLAH. I just sat there thinking, "So what? That means nothing to me. I won't become a victim to breast cancer!" How wrong could I have been?

I sobbed in my husband's arms. THIS WAS NOT SUPPOSED TO HAVE HAPPENED! I began to doubt the power of positive thinking, to doubt myself, as well as life and the injustice that had just been thrown at me.

Once I reluctantly accepted the reality of my situation, it was time to see what had to be done, as it was time to rid my body of this unwanted intruder. It had created so much vulnerability, uncertainty, fear, and pain not only for myself also for my husband John, my family and friends, and I just had to confront it. I didn't want to die! Then the adrenaline set in; it was time to take action to get rid of this intruder! We scheduled the subsequent surgery. War had been declared... Let the battle begin!

The evening after I received my diagnosis, I couldn't sleep so in the middle of the night I went up and sat on the couch totally alone, in the stillness and the darkness of the moment, I contemplated my future. I had been planning my 50th birthday party and was determined that I was going to celebrate it. I thought of all the future weddings, birthdays, Christmas's, Easters, anniversaries in my life and in the lives of my loved ones. I wanted to live! I had too much to do, to experience, and to live for. From that moment on, I realized that it would be one day at a time, and every day was precious.

On the day of my surgery, I underwent a procedure where they injected me with nuclear dye to trace where the cancer was. I was about to be wheeled into the operatig theatre when my surgeon mentioned that some dye was detected around my lung area, and she did not know what she would find until she operated. Tears ran down my face as I was being anesthetized, not knowing what I would wake up to... a missing breast? Being told that the cancer had spread to all of my body? Having this disease made me feel so alone, so helpless, and yet so desperate to cling to life... while John was left to wait and see what was going to happen to his wife.

Thank God I... ® *Am an Empowered Woman:*

I woke up in pain wearing a blood-stained gown, John by my side in a room filled with flowers... still alive and feeling loved very much! Where to now? The operation was a success! I was very blessed as they had found the cancer at its earliest stages, even though it was aggressive. Only a quarter of my right breast had been removed, and thankfully, the cancer had not spread into my lungs or lymph nodes.

Now it was time to work out my recovery and the best way to deal with the situation at hand. The surgeon and nurse took both John and I aside and explained what we should be considering in aiding my recovery, to ensure that the cancer would not reoccur. They suggested that I take a course of cancer treatment drugs for the next five years and strongly recommended that I undergo eight weeks of radiotherapy, as they were confident that they had eradicated the cancer in my body. The surgeon placed no real urgency on the radiotherapy treatment other than to say that she highly recommended it.

This caused consternation in John; he was fearful of my filling my body with drugs and radiation. I, however, was determined to do whatever it took to rid my body of this intruder. John said, "Nilla, the surgeon has told you that she took all the cancer away. You no longer have cancer." I replied that I would do what I needed to do to stay alive and that I wanted to undergo radiation treatment. I thought the only option was to fill my body with drugs, just in case there was a rogue cancer cell running around inside my body. All I wanted to do was to take action. As they say, with every action there is an equal and opposite reaction. The conflict between my determination to do what I thought was right for me, and John's frustration at watching me suffer began to take its toll on our relationship immediately.

On the first day of my radiotherapy treatment, John drove me to Perth and that night flew to Vancouver to be with his son. This was his way of showing me that I was fine. I was devastated the person I loved the most in my life had left me to face this challenge on my own...

The doctors, specialists, and surgeon had all reassured us that the cancer had been taken out of my body and that continuing with treatment was only a precaution and in the end, my choice.

John left me to face my first day of treatment on my own with an angel of a girlfriend. As I walked into the treatment room all I saw was a lone table in a huge room, with machines everywhere. I burst into tears! I felt so alone, so vulnerable, and so scared! I knew I had to be brave, as I had a fight on my hands, and I was going to be the victor. No one could win this war for me; I had to do it, with or without John's support.

While I underwent my radiotherapy, I was told by a fellow breast cancer survivor to be mindful of allowing depression to set in. What was she talking about? That was not going to happen to me! But depression had already crept into my life. I had become irrational and cried all the time. I felt like I'd lost my personality, and I was slowly losing myself. My family and friends merely tolerated my behaviour because they loved me, and our staff would have left our business if they'd had any other place to work. John stood by and watched as the person that he loved slowly destroyed herself, when in essence, there was no need.

He knew that this would happen, he just had to let me do what I felt was right for me, despite how hard he tried to make it different. Could it have been that I had allowed the depression to set in and that I subconsciously decided it was going to serve me, and that I didn't deserve anything more? Could it have been that watching John stand beside me, loving me even though he was watching me destroy myself; when I realised that something had to change? Could it have been by chance that I was open to what happened next...

An email from John arrived in my inbox in February 2006, suggesting that we attend a personal development weekend. It asked if our lives, health, and wealth were where we wanted them to be, and suggested that if not, we should consider attending the seminar. I suddenly realized that our relationship had reached the breaking point when I saw that my husband had sent me an email when we were within an arm's distance from each other! Our ability to communicate was gone. Our communication skills had become so bad that John couldn't even talk to me. My immediate response to the email was "Yes! My life, health, and wealth are *desperately* in need of improvement!"

I thought to myself. Could my emotions about our relationship be affecting my life so deeply that I let it affect my health? Could opening my heart and listening to those who loved me help me heal my body?

In April 2006, we attended a personal development seminar, which changed my entire life. How could two days change my life forever? During the weekend, I realized that I alone have control over every outcome in my life! John saw such a difference over those two days that he did not hesitate to invest $17,000 for me to continue learning about how powerful the mind is and that everything starts from within. As he signed the contract for me to attend subsequent courses, we looked into each other's eyes and he uttered these words, "Nilla, this is your 50th birthday present." What a huge gift it was!

Over the next six months I learned to take responsibility for the results in my life and to understand that the mind is the most powerful thing that I possess. Once the mind is stretched it can never go back to where it was.

John gave me a precious gift, a gift of love, of understanding and ultimately the gift of the life that I have today.

Thank God I have survived and thrived from breast cancer because today I live in gratitude for a husband that truly loves me. Because of my experience with breast cancer, I am now able to help others. My hard-won message is that the most important thing is to not get caught up in being a victim to cancer. Cancer is not a death sentence! Having had cancer created opportunities for me to learn, to grow, and to live without fear, without regrets, and without expectations.

There were many times when both John and I could have given up, there were many times that I wanted to end my life, there were times when John wanted to walk out of the darkness that the cancer and depression caused! The miracle of love is what saw me get through to what seemed to be an impossible dream, the dream of a normal life, with the one I love...John.

With the "miracle of love" I am now able to live my passion each and every day. I also live my purpose each and every day, which is to lead, inspire and make a difference in people's lives through travel and travel experiences.

It is through travelling, meeting people, understanding cultures, and having the desire to learn and grow personally

Thank God I... [R] *Am an Empowered Woman:*

that has created an open mindedness to what can be achieved and what is possible.

www.TravelwithPurpose.com.au

Thank God I Felt the Love Bond Between a Mother and Her Child
By Lia Enso

The first time I felt a twinge in my tummy it was so slight I barely noticed it.

I was busy greeting guests in a capacity filled room at the waterfront restaurant. The sun was just setting over the water, casting a warm orange glow throughout the mahogany floored lounge that overlooked the Marina. The air buzzed with the energy of the cocktail set. A three member jazz band played in the corner by the fireplace as people danced and mingled about. It was holiday time and everyone was full of good cheer at the annual year-end mixer.

I was enjoying the festive atmosphere and seeing all the smiling faces when I felt another twinge. This time it was unmistakable. It soon progressed to a dull ache in my stomach. I wondered if it was something I ate. Perhaps all the excitement and planning for the various holiday events was just catching up to me. I took a big sip of the sparkling water I'd been drinking hoping it would settle my stomach and all would be well. It didn't help. My stomach refused to settle. The ache got heavier and more insistent. Then suddenly, the dull pain turned sharp. My heart began to race. I rushed to the bathroom.

That's when I saw the brownish red stain on my panties. Instead of panicking, I found myself calmly wrapping several sheets of toilet paper and placing them over the stain. My mind wasn't making the connection because I wouldn't allow it. I heard familiar voices outside the stall asking me if everything was ok. I heard myself answer, "Everything's just fine. I'll be out in a moment."

I was about to walk out back to the party, when I felt another sharp pain. My heart again started racing. I knew then I had to leave. All I would allow my mind to think about was getting home. I stood in the stall and waited for what felt like an eternity until all the voices in the bathroom dissipated. I snuck out and left the holiday party without a word to anyone.

As soon as I walked in the door, I dropped my purse on the floor and crawled into my bed in a fetal position. The pain was coming in waves now, at times so intense, all I could do was close my eyes and focus on breathing. Up until that point in my life, I had rarely suffered any acute physical pain, so I did not have any Tylenol, Motrin or any other type of pain killer in my home. The only thing I had was my breath to help alleviate any pain. I took deep breaths in and out, in and out. I could hear my cell ringing in my purse. There would be a pause after several rings and then it would start again, over and over.

I lay in my bed, unable to move. I was miscarrying.

It occurred to me that I should get to the emergency room, but the thought soon passed as I was overcome with another wave of intense pain and became focused entirely again on just breathing. The stronger the pain, the more I focused on my breath. After years of meditation, it was what my body was conditioned to do. I also, quite frankly, had no alternative then, but to breathe and stay calm.

I could feel blood beginning to flow out of me. I knew I had to get to the bathroom, but I could not get my body upright. I rolled myself out of bed tucked in a fetal position and dropped to the floor. I took a deep breath, mustering whatever strength I could and started crawling to the bathroom. Every few strides, I had to stop to just be still and breathe as the contractions became more intense.

When I finally got to the bathroom, the pain was so excruciating, I thought I might pass out and bleed to death right there on the tile, still in my cocktail dress. I was groaning and making noises I'd never heard out of me before. My heart was pounding, and I was drenched in sweat. I was having a hard time now catching my breath. My mind went fuzzy, and I heard myself praying to God to please just let me go, please let me go to escape the pain.

Then the words of Thich Nhat Hanh came to me, words that I'd read many times in the past. "When you are dealing with pain, do not fight against pain. Embrace it with great tenderness as though you were embracing a little baby." I don't know whether the pain just got so great that I became numb, but somehow I was able to get up off the floor, take my clothes off, and sit myself on the toilet.

My body then did what it needed to do. I delivered my baby. It was done.
It was stunning how quickly and how thoroughly all the physical pain went away. Literally, in an instant.

In that very moment, I experienced such a dichotomy of feelings both in spirit and body that I have never experienced in my life. In that exact moment when the precious being I had been carrying for nearly 16 weeks left my body, I felt tremendous gratitude, release, and relief from the excruciating physical pain I'd been enduring and at the same time felt the overwhelming, unbearable heartache and emotional pain for the loss of my baby. I was so thankful to

God for taking the physical pain away and in utter despair for losing life.

One moment I carried life and in the next, it was gone, just like that. In that moment, nothing mattered at all. Everything that had seemed important to me... my family, my friends, everything that I had worked so hard for, my education, my career, and my relationships were now meaningless.

I sat there on the toilet, my head bowed, hands cradling my face, crying for another couple of hours.

After there were no more tears to cry, my entire being having been spent and emptied, a realization came over me in the void. An intrinsic, ineffable knowing and feeling filled me deeply within my core that I have a hard time even today, ascribing it to words. This spirit that had entered my physical body and left in physical form was still there, connected, deep within me. I felt it in the energy of the cells in my body. The love didn't go away.

Even though it was only for a short while, I was the mother to this precious being. This baby gave me the gift of knowing what pure, unconditional love means, and I am grateful for that. I mourn the loss but I am awakened, transformed, and alive because of how intensely I felt the bond between us.

My baby is gone, but the love remains today, warm in my heart.

I hope by telling my story, I can encourage others to share their stories. I have been encouraged and supported by women who have also experienced miscarriage. For many, it is a silent sorrow. No one quite knows what to say or do to comfort us, even those who are the closest — our husbands, partners, family and friends. It is hard for many women to ask for help, we often don't know what we need. Sometimes it's just easier not to say anything and move on as if nothing happened. After all, as they say, it wasn't a real baby. But for the countless women who experience miscarriage (especially those past the first trimester), the bond is real, the love is real, and the life is real — it is our baby. I encourage those inspired who have gone through a similar experience to give yourself the gift (freedom) in honoring in whatever form that feels right, the loving spirit that you carried in your womb, however long or short the duration. Fully experiencing and knowing this blessing is truly the most beautiful gift.

All my love, Lia.

♥♥♥

Lia is a writer, healer and mother. In writing her story, she hopes to encourage others who have experienced miscarriage to share their stories.

enso@touchofenso.com
www.touchofenso.com

Thank God I Hated Myself
By Mary Ann Swanson

The trailer was so small. And when he hit me, it seemed even smaller.

I scanned the hovel we called home and tried not to focus on the throbbing pain that spewed out of my fresh bruises. What kind of life did I have? How did this happen? I could hear engines roaring through our thin walls, but it became background noise in the midst of my daydreaming. I saw myself as a young girl trying to navigate my way through the demons that haunted me back then. The dirty dishes in front of me and the squeakiness under my feet became obsolete as I mentally revisited my past.

As a child, I was very strong-willed and stubborn, always wanting to follow my own course. My parents and teachers felt that I didn't fit into what they thought I should be. They tried very hard to make me conform to their expectations, but the harder they tried, the more I rebelled. Out of frustration, my parents and my teachers told me I would never amount to anything and no matter what I did it would never be good enough! They thought the best way to save me was through tough love. I only saw a fight, and I fought back.

Then when I was 14, I was devastated when my church leaders segregated me and called me the devil in front of my Sunday school class. That was my last straw. All the people who were my authority figures, the people I looked up to, were saying I was no good and was totally worthless.

I thought they must be right, and that's when I gave up. I felt unloved and alone. I found myself despair, struck to my core with painful, aching misery, longing to be done and to remove myself from this world! That is when I fully committed to hating myself and all others. I believed everyone was out to get me, so I decided I would get them first. I was so deeply lost in a dark pit of self-loathing that for many years I was unable to see if there even could be good in others.

I did everything possible I could think of to take me off this planet. My life motto became "Live fast, die young, and leave a beautiful corpse." Damn any rules or so-called authority that would stop me from my joyride. Because of the people I chose to surround myself with, I had multiple near-death experiences, extremely dangerous encounters with fast cars and drunk driving. I almost went to jail, and yet still, nothing would change my mind about this godforsaken place I was stuck in.

Not long after this, he came into the picture. Because he was one of the guys that was in my crowd, I suppose it made sense that we got together. After we had dated for a while, he dared me to prove my love for him by leaving everything I knew. Feeling desperate to be loved, I obeyed. I left it all behind — my family, my friends, and my freedom. I walked out on the life I knew and into a life of homelessness, fear, and abuse.

He controlled me. He told me what I could and couldn't do. He kept my keys so I couldn't use my car without his approval. He'd laugh at me and use my own fears against me. I once told him I didn't like cigarette smoke, so he held me down, blew smoke in my face, and laughed. Often we didn't have a place to live or food to eat. Some days I was uncertain where I would sleep, whether I would eat, or which of my fears would be used to torment me. He hit me and yelled at me and told me I was worthless. He said that I was a piece of crap and shouldn't be alive. I agreed.

One day he looked at me and told me we were done. He said he had another girlfriend. It was fun while it lasted, but I was worthless, and he didn't want me around anymore. He spat in my face and told me to get out. I had nothing left and nowhere to go. My body went numb inside. Blackness descended over me. I had nothing because I had given everything away. Complete emptiness.

I walked right out into the street, nothing but a shell. You could hear the roaring sounds of a dump truck speeding around the corner. It was already decided. I was going to take my life right then and there. Just a few more seconds and I wouldn't have to feel the pain anymore. I proceeded forward, but he came from behind and yanked me back to safety, reprimanding my stupidity.

Of course I stayed with him after that. It was hell being with him, but it was the only place I had.

Another month of abuse rolled by.

The blasting of a horn outside interrupted my walk down memory lane, and I realized it was time to pick him up from work. Now I understood what kind of life I had and how it happened. I lived in a dump with a spiteful man. And those church people used to call me the devil!

As we were driving back to our trailer, I decided to confront him. I don't know if it was recalling the experiences of my past or just remembering that I have always been a fighter, but I was ready to go back to my family. This obviously irritated him and his anger only seemed to escalate as we got closer to home. Once we arrived back at our shack, I attempted to pack my things. That's when he burst through the door in a fit of utter rage proclaiming that I would never leave.

A dark shroud of inhuman hatred consumed him. He was no longer the man I knew, but a predator, living off the hunt. He forced me on the bed, pinned me down and tried to shove a sock in my mouth and a pillow over my face. "I'm going to rape you and you're going to enjoy every minute of it!" He yelled. The strike of a match could be heard through the pillow. I panicked. "You're mine! Even if I have to take you to eternity, then you'll be mine forever!" He roared.

That was it. There was no way I was going to die with him. I would survive at any cost. I fought with everything inside of me, desperately clawing and scratching at whatever I could find.

He backhanded me across the face, splitting my lip. My tongue immediately recognized the iron flavor that flowed from my gash. Still fighting, I pleaded to the powers that be. I thought to myself if there is a god, please, let me live. Give me a second chance. I swear I will change. I promise.

Continuing to cling onto my survival, in the midst of all the chaos that was happening around me, a great force suddenly came over me, and I was filled with the will to live. In one powerful shove, he was flung across the trailer, flying backwards seven feet into the air. It was absolutely impossible, yet here it was, in the blink of an eye, a supernatural phenomenon.

It was as though some sort of mysterious ethereal energy had picked him up from his collar and flung him like a bug off a leaf. He was on his knees shaking and in shock! "What the hell just happened? How the hell did you do that? What are you? Some kind of witch?!" He hollered. Confidence pulsed through my blood, mixed with pure adrenaline. I looked him straight in the eye and said, "I don't know if it was me, but I know someone is definitely looking out for me."

Something inside me finally woke up, and I ran. I ran to save my life.

As I stormed out of that trailer, the lyrics of "Already Gone" by The Eagles filled the air. "Well I know it wasn't you who held me down... Heaven knows it wasn't you who set me free... So oftentimes it happens that we live our lives in chains... And we never even know we have the key."

Mary Ann Swanson, co-author with Thank God I am an Empowered Women book series (Thank God I Hated Myself), co-hosted an internet radio talk show. Certified both as a Prema Birthing Practitioner and Angel Attunement facilitator, she works with her team of angels and the celestial realms as a powerful pure channel of spiritual wisdom and inspiration. And now she's certified as a oneness blessings giver too!

Thank God I Was Adopted
By Sarah Collinge

The atmosphere crackles with anticipation in the delivery room. Everyone present seems to share a supercharged alertness, brought about by the new life emerging from this soon-to-be mother. And her very loud voice.

She screams again. This one is the worst yet.

My responsibility as a Registered Nurse overrides my impulse to focus on pity, and I check the woman's vital signs. As I witness her agony in this last push, the empathetic part of me can't help wishing she had gotten an epidural to help with the pain, if not for herself then for me.

But as an actor, I'm always observing, and there's a passionate part of me that is filing this away for later use. I find human behavior immensely fascinating, and I love to use what I learn in my craft. Today this sweat-soaked Jane Doe with anxiety etched across her face has given me some real insight. If I ever play the part of a woman in labor after seeing this, get that Oscar ready!

But what happens next is something I'm just not ready for.

I wipe the copious scarlet from the tiny face of the newborn, and put seven pounds, four ounces of pure vulnerability into the mother's arms. Her countenance transforms as I watch all her misery turning into bliss before me. There is tightness in my chest, and I'm suddenly overcome.

In her eyes, I see all the feeling she has for her child, and I know I'm in the presence of something boundless.

Something timeless. What I'm gazing into is an abyss of love.

"Sarah." I hear my name as though from far away. And then more sharply. "Sarah!"

When I look up at the doctor, my eyes are stinging. He stares at me in surprise. He knows I'm adept at keeping my emotions in check. I slap a tear away as I flee the room, blindsided by feelings I have never dealt with.

How could my birth mother have given me away? And why?

My adoptive parents were cautious when the Agency informed them that a baby girl had just been born to a 17-year-old and was up for adoption.

"I'm not sure I can go through it all again," my adoptive mother said. Six months earlier they had adopted twins, Sarah and Simon. But their birth mother had changed her mind, and they'd had to give them back after 2 weeks of thinking they were a new family. It was heartbreaking.

But as this new baby gazed up at them, they knew there was no going back. "Can you promise us this adoption will be final?" my adoptive father had asked. The Agency promised.

Theirs had been a true love story. My father was an officer in the Royal Air Force and Mum was a nurse. They met one Sunday in the crypt of St Clement Danes church when they were both on duty. Dad proposed a week later and they were married within 4 months. They dearly wanted to start a family but couldn't conceive, and so they decided to adopt.

They took me home with them at 5 weeks old, chose a new name for me, and loved me as their very own. I was their daughter, and they couldn't have loved me more if I had been born of them. I was secure and happy growing up as an only child, and unaware of the significance of my adoption. Like most children, I just lived in the moment and got on with the business of growing up. My parents told me that being adopted made me special, and that sounded good enough to me!

My parents and I love each other unconditionally, yet I'm also aware they are not my flesh and blood. I have never looked into any face that resembles mine. No one is able to say how much like Auntie-so-and-so I am, or predict my future talents and tendencies according to family history.

Since my epiphany in the delivery room, I cannot stop the questions from coming. Who am I? Where did I come from? Do my birth parents think about me? What is my genetic inheritance?

At 24, after much deliberation, I contact the Adoption Agency. They tell me my birth mother had hoped I would come looking for her one day, and had registered her details years ago.

"Hello," I stammer into the phone's receiver. "This is your daughter..." The words are not easy to say and they echo strangely in my head. I feel a twinge of disloyalty and I correct myself, "... your birth daughter."

After she put me up for adoption, my biological mother had gone on to have two other children. I have a half brother and sister. She had also become a nurse! My biological father had gone on to become a doctor, and a grandfather and uncle are also doctors. Is it any wonder that I was drawn toward nursing? What strange coincidences! My mind is reeling with new information. I'm getting a sense of my genetic inheritance already, and it's a lot to digest.

Still intensely curious, I go alone to the meeting place.

"Geraldine," I hear someone call, and I take no notice. But it comes again more insistently, from behind me. "Geraldine!"

I turn and look into a face more similar to my own than any I have ever seen before. She takes my hand in hers, and it is so much like mine that it's almost spooky. I feel a primal attraction to her that is completely reflexive and involuntary.

"I've dreamt of this moment for so long," she says.

But even with this visceral urge to embrace my own flesh and blood at last, I feel emotionally torn. There, in her eyes, is that look of boundless maternal love I saw on that woman's face in the delivery room.
She steps forward and puts her arms around me, tears welling up.

Now I have what I thought I had come here seeking. Here is that pure, unrelenting, limitless parental adoration... and for some unknown reason I stand here wooden, deflecting it.

I pull back, look again into my birth mother's love-struck eyes, and suddenly I'm angry.

"If you cared this much, then why?"

"One night, my mother heard me crying and came into my room. I'd been trying to conceal the pregnancy because I didn't know what to do," my birth mother tells me. "You'd better leave home before your father finds out!" her own mother had said. So she left her hometown and was sent to a Mother and Baby home miles away, to give birth.

"I knew I was considered too young to bring up a child on my own and back then it was taboo to be an unmarried mother. Your father was only 18, and we decided there was little choice but to put you up for adoption. It was an agony but we thought you would have a better life."

I can't argue with this. It has proven to be true.

"Did you ever... regret it?" I ask.

"Three weeks later, I tried to get you back," she continues, "But they wouldn't take you away from the couple who adopted you. They said they had made a special promise. I was distraught."

I know she had loved me and thought about me over the years, and I feel deep compassion for her as a young mum having to part with her baby. She did the best she could at the time in the most difficult of circumstances.

"Why are you still so angry?" she asks. The question catches me off guard.

"Because you look at me like only a mother can look at her child," I blurt. "You look at me with a love that only a parent can feel."

"Yes," she replies, "that is how I look at you."

"The thing that makes this hard for me," I tell her, "is that it's familiar. It's the look my Mum gave me night and day as I tumbled through childhood. I had that. She was there, and she gave it to me."

"But I have it for you... too," her words trail off. In this moment, my birth mother understands that in every sense I already have great parents, and I can't be someone else's daughter as well. I can't fulfill her dream of stepping into my life and filling a void. There is no void.

"I should not have called you Geraldine," she says. "Your name is Sarah, and I'll just have to accept that."

"No," I tell her, "'Geraldine' isn't *who* I am, nor is 'Sarah'. I am the sum total of all my experiences *and* my genetic makeup. But most important of all, I am who I choose to be."

"And who do you choose to be, dear?" my birth mother asks me.

"I'm an actress, mother," I reply, but she doesn't hear my words. She's transfixed by my facial expression. I've already used my skills to conjure up a nice parting gift for this woman who gave me life. I look at her with a love in my eyes that only a daughter can feel for her mother.

I've had a good life, and I love my parents very much. I'm blessed to have been given a stable home life where I felt safe and loved. I don't know who I might have become if I had been brought up by my 17-year-old mum, and I will never know. It was a healing process to find out more about my origins, but I couldn't change the past. I had been given unconditional love by my parents and just as I had been a gift to them, I feel they have been a gift to me.

Meeting my birth mother hasn't changed who I am. It has given me a different perspective on my life though. It was an amazing experience but it gradually began to dawn on me that I needn't have been asking, 'Who am I?' just because I was adopted, because who I am now is who I choose to be.

I choose to see the universe as a perfect place wherein everything has a purpose and there are no mistakes. I choose to honor life in all its different forms and to marvel at the universal intelligence that holds it all together perfectly. I trust my instincts, my inner promptings, and feel guided in all my undertakings by something greater than myself.

I developed a passion for acting, and in every character I portray, I draw on the experiences of my soul, but with my feet firmly on the ground. All of life is a stage in a sense, and acting is a perfect medium for me to express the different aspects of myself in a purposeful and creative way. I may be asked to be Geraldine or Sarah or Ruth or Jennifer, and I can become any of them for a film, but I always feel the 'me' inside, and I know that's who I am! I also feel passionate about helping others to help themselves by sharing in any small way what I have learnt along the way. I live for the moment and am grateful for all that I do have and don't dwell on all that I don't have or could have had.

Who am I? I am all that I am!

It was Mother's Day and I took Mum a big bunch of her favorite lilies. "Thank you for adopting me, Mum, and loving me through thick and thin. I'm sorry you and Dad weren't able to have a child together, you know, your own flesh and blood. Has it ever bothered you?"

"No, darling, it never has. I can honestly say that it's never made a lot of difference to me that I didn't carry you for nine months. As far as I was concerned you were my daughter from the moment I laid eyes on you and nothing will ever change that. We've had our ups and downs like any other mother and daughter but once a mum, always a mum, even when your kids are grown up. You'll understand that yourself now that you're a mum too."

She is, no doubt, a warm and lovely person, but she wasn't the one who was there for me every night and day as I tumbled through childhood. She isn't the one I called "Mummy."

I was born Geraldine Ann Pimblett to an unmarried teenager and adopted at 5 weeks old by a mature couple and re-named Sarah Jane Collinge. At 21, I qualified as a Nurse and went on to work in London, America, and Australia. I love to write and act and currently have a lead role in a feature film. I have two sons.

Thank God I Am an Empowered Woman
By Olivia Parr-Rud

Someone pinch me! Is it possible? Have I really made it? Here I am, sitting at a small table in the CEO's office, waiting for the meeting to start. The view is breathtaking! Through a huge corner window I can see the ocean, the bay, and Golden Gate Bridge.

This is my first meeting with the elite management team. It's still hard to believe. Have I broken through the glass ceiling? After all, I am participating in one of 'those' meetings – meetings to which very few are invited... meetings where *real* decisions are made. And I'd like to point out that I am the only female. But I am overwhelmed with self-doubt. Almost paralyzed... Will these men respect me as a peer? Will they value my ideas? Do I belong here? How did I get here?

Until six months ago, I lived a very different life. Granted, I had a brief stint with a finance company right out of college. But I quickly left that world and spent the next 18 years being what is best described as a 'Granola Mom.' While managing a household with three small kids, I found my passion in the study of psychology and spirituality. I never imagined myself back in the corporate world as a statistician. I'm finding this difficult to manage. My husband's health is failing. I'm struggling to keep my family together. And now, as the newly promoted Director of Acquisition, I am responsible for 95% of the bank's income. I should be thrilled. But I'm terrified. Will my talent for numbers see me through this?

Thank God I...® Am an Empowered Woman:

Within two months of arriving at the bank, I developed a set of statistical models that saved them $37 million a year by more accurately identifying people who responded to their high-rate credit card offers. Sometimes I think I just got lucky. Credit cards were taking off. Computer power was quickly advancing. Data was plentiful. You could say that I was in the right place at the right time with the right skill set. But I think what gave me the real edge was my creativity. I was always trying new ways to develop models that were outside the rules of statistics. And they worked. They saved my company millions of dollars. And now I'm considered a superstar....

So here I am, in this meeting with the top leaders of the bank. I look around, taking in all the glory of making it. All that hard work and struggle has paid off. I guess this is my new tribe. But something doesn't feel quite right. They all appear very stiff in their 3-piece suits and aggressive postures. They look like they're prepping for the hunt... Are the consumers their prey?

The conversation begins. Am I really hearing this? "I suggest we add extra interest if they don't use their card. If we only mention it in the 'Change in Terms,' the customer won't even notice it. It could increase revenues by millions," said one of the team members. My mind starts spinning. I'm trying to stay engaged. But I can't hide the horror on my face. I can't believe these guys are so matter of fact about fleecing their customers.

I'm trying to understand their point of view. But something doesn't feel right. Are they really that heartless? Do they have no respect or compassion for their customers? These men are discussing how to word the fine print in the credit card offer so that it was intentionally confusing! I'm shocked. My eyes widen. I feel my body contracting. I look around hoping no one notices me. I feel myself shutting down. If I don't, I fear that I'll start crying.

I'm beginning to realize that I am miserable. This place is the antithesis of spiritual. It feels so alien. But I have to stay. I have to support my family. But how do I act? What are my choices?

After days of soul searching, I finally feel at peace within myself. I think I've found a way to survive. I've come to a decision. I have to be true to my core beliefs... my spiritual values. I don't have to preach. I don't even have to say anything. I just have to live it. I will *be* spiritual. I will live my daily life from a deeply spiritual place. I'll make every decision from a place of love. That's the only way I can keep my sanity.

Flash forward fifteen years. My skills are the hottest on the planet. I've written a best-selling book on data mining. I've worked or consulted for nearly every large financial institution and technology company, including Wal-Mart, SAS, HP, Xerox, IBM, Cisco, Wells Fargo, Citizens Bank, State Farm, Nationwide, et cetera. I've delivered keynotes and lectures at over 200 venues worldwide. I'm now considered an expert in business intelligence (BI) – defined as computer-based techniques used in identifying, accessing, and analyzing business data, related to marketing, risk and/or operations within a department or function of a business. But I'm sitting here feeling very empty inside.

It's early in the morning... very dark and quiet. I'm preparing for my meditation. I feel so lost. I ask for guidance. "What am I doing here? Why am I trapped in the corporate world? It feels so awful... so cold and alien." A response comes through so clearly... "This is where you need to be to learn the skills to do your *real* work." I have no idea what this means. What is my *real* work?

I'm excited! Today I got a sign. Out of the blue, I received an email from the largest privately owned software company in the world, inviting me to deliver a keynote address at their international business intelligence conference in Las Vegas. My guess is that they want me to talk about business intelligence. I do, too. But not the way they define it. What has become clear to me over the years, what I'm discovering is my *real* work, is the importance of the human component of business intelligence.

Oh sure... the technology is a big part of it. But it's not all of it. After many years of working with and for people who lead from their hearts, I feel that I know what drives success. I know what inspires greatness. I want to talk about the business intelligence that is generated by the human brain... and heart... when humans are empowered to fully show up and express themselves to their fullest potential.

I'm feeling pretty courageous at the moment. But what exactly will I say? How can I frame my message?

Suddenly I recall that traumatic meeting at the bank. The cold, dehumanizing men who had no compassion for their customers. Are they my audience? Probably the majority of it. I know I can't appeal to their feelings. It seems like they mainly care about making a profit. How can I craft a message that inspires them to treat people better by appealing to their pocketbooks?

I have an idea. I'll combine some key elements from my early lectures on communication, collaboration and leadership. These are the skills that really drive success, especially in companies that leverage business intelligence. I'll call it "Business Intelligence Success Factors."

Now I have to create my slides. This is really stressful. I'm really struggling with how to deliver my message...

Ah, I have an idea! I'll write about the science! I'll compare Newtonian Physics to Quantum Physics. Newtonian physics is very linear, driven by cause and effect. Quantum physics views everything as a system with many interrelated parts. Businesses are systems comprised of many interrelated parts. This should be easy!

Only three days until the big day. I'm feeling very nervous. What will I wear? Should I wear a black pants suit? Should I try to look like them? That doesn't feel right. I want to fit in. But I don't want to hide. My message *is* different. I can't be afraid to look different. I think I'll wear my burgundy silk pants suit. The design is quite feminine. I know I'll be comfortable in that. All these decisions are driving me crazy.

I'M STILL ON THE PLANE – TRYING TO RELAX – GET MORE IDEAS – MAYBE QUANTUM PHYSICS ISN'T THE WAY TO GO – STILL IN A PANIC – THEN ANOTHER IDEA COMES – LAST MINUTE DECISIONS – CAN BE BRILLIANT – CAN FALL FLAT. BIG RISK. KEEP THEM IN SUSPENSE – THE PERSON NEXT TO ME ASKS IF I'M OKAY.

There's something about flying that brings out the little kid in me. I always want a window seat so I can watch the land as it retreats. The people disappear. The cars look like little ants scurrying around. The waterways appear as glistening ribbons. I could look out the window and daydream for hours. But I have this big event tomorrow. I must refocus.

Thank God I... ® *Am an Empowered Woman:*

I'm beginning to have some real doubts about my approach to this presentation.

To prepare for my talk, I'm reading a book by Patricia Aburdene called *Megatrends 2010* (Hampton Roads Publishing, 2007). All of a sudden I realize that my presentation is all wrong. Maybe quantum physics isn't the way to go... I can just imagine their eyes glazing over. They're asking themselves, "What the h... is she talking about?" I'm delivering it tomorrow afternoon! And I've already sent in my slides. A sense of panic sets in.

Okay, slow down. Breathe... My mind is racing. I start taking notes. I'm tempted to start reconstructing my slides. But I don't want to act too hastily. I have to figure this out. Am I rejecting my original approach too quickly? Or did I stumble upon the right information just in time?

As I'm reading Patricia's book, I realize that my presentation is trying to appeal to their logical mind. In a way, I'm selling out. Sure, I want everything to make sense. But I also want them to 'feel' something... be inspired. Patricia has the perfect data for that. Now I'm anxious to get to my hotel room and start reworking my presentation.

I'm awestruck! My room is spectacular! It's a 1500 square foot suite with a 180 degree curved window around the living and dining area. I have the perfect place to work at the dining room table. And I can look out and see the bluish-gray mountains. I feel so supported by the universe.

Now I'm excited to get started. My new plan seems convincing. I think I'll just start from scratch. I feel so comfortable here. I'll just dedicate the rest of the evening and tomorrow morning to revamping my presentation.

As the time for my keynote approaches, I feel a combination of excitement and dread. This is the biggest and perhaps bravest I've ever felt. Well, I haven't done it yet. But it's going to happen. That's for sure.

As the host introduces me, my knees start to knock a little. I do some visualization to ground myself. I feel the energy of the room. There are several hundred people out there. It's exciting and terrifying all at the same time. I walk out to the podium.

"Good afternoon! Today, I'm going to talk about a new kind of business intelligence. We all know that the world of business is changing at a rapid rate..."

Right now, I feel like I'm out of my body... like I am watching myself. I'm talking to the audience and having a conversation in my head at the same time. I feel like I'm witnessing myself.

The energy in the room feels receptive. I sense that some are fully receiving what I'm saying. I sense that others are confused, perhaps even hostile. My sense is that I am speaking to their hearts. That may be challenging for some. Telsus Mobility (6,000 employees, $2.6 billion in sales), embraced a commitment to Wellness.

The organization supports popular, spiritually based workshops to boost energy decision making ability, productivity, responsibility, reflection and self-esteem. From 1999 to 2000, the use of wellness services rose 47%. The cost of prescription drugs and sick time dropped 16%. 92% of TELSUS Mobility employees agree with the statement: 'I am responsible for contributing to our profitability.'"

Thank God I... ® *Am an Empowered Woman:*

Now I'm noticing more people really paying attention. This feels good. I think they're getting it.

"American Express took on a project where three vice presidents and 13 financial advisors from the Upstate New York Marketing Group signed on for a year's training in emotional competence, stress management and forgiveness. After one year, stress fell 25%, positive feelings rose 20%, sales were 60% higher than other groups."

"HeartMath's Inner Quality Management program provides feedback on how thoughts and emotions affect the heart rate. Used by more than 100 companies, including Hewlett-Packard, BP, Cisco, Boeing, Motorola and Liz Claiborne, showing a customer service unit of Fortune 50 company reduced stress by 50% and improved customer listening by 33%; a healthcare firm reduced turnover by 50%, raised customer satisfaction 27%, saved $1.5 million in two years and was ranked #1 nationwide in employee satisfaction; 75% of executives saw dramatic improvements in performance, resilience, health, and leadership."

"MEDITATION – Chemical manufacturer in Detroit offered Transcendental Meditation training. 3 years later, almost 75% of employees were still meditating. Absenteeism fell 85. Injuries dropped 70%. Sick days decreased 76%. Productivity soared 120%."

Now the room feels very different. My sense is that these amazing results appeal to their hearts and their accountants.

"Every company can benefit from offering training in the softer skills. And wouldn't it be great to be able to bring your whole self to work? To let your creative mind expand and play?

Awakening Your Inner Strength and Genius...

"What if you really felt valued by your team? Your boss?

"What if you felt truly inspired in your workplace every day?

"Namaste."

The applause is intoxicating. I feel like I've bared my heart and soul.

A few minutes later, the editor-in-chief of SAS Publishing approaches me to see if I would be interested in writing a book on this topic. I'm thinking, "Really? You want me to write about this? I have no credentials in this area... ." Then I get it. This is what I'm supposed to do. This is the reward for a lifetime of passionate study — study of what really drives success. Yes, this is my *real* work.

Now that I've have found my voice, I'm seeking ways to show up in the world where it can support me.

My main business is still primarily statistical work. But my research over the last seven years has been in the link between our fast-paced, high-tech, global economy and the importance of the human factor. In my latest book, *Business Intelligence Success Factors* (Wiley/SAS 2009), I link the importance of human competencies to business success through models in science and nature. Yes, I have found my voice. Now is the time to be heard. Thank God I am an Empowered Woman.

Thank God I Was Ugly
By Tina Marie Jones

I adjust my mic pack, smooth out my dress, then stroll through the drafty hallway toward the set. Two minutes left before lights... camera... action!

"Lucy... you have some 'splaining' to do," one producer yells out to the tech hand nearest me. It's always hectic during the final moments before going live.

I turn to face a floor-length mirror, glancing over my attire, hair, and makeup one last time before making my entrance. Mirrors and I never used to get along. But today, I no longer see that awkward girl who stuck out like a sore thumb among her peers. A light giggle escapes my lips, and with a sly grin, I slowly eyeball my every curve. "Girl, how did you ever think you were ugly?"

Me, ugly? I have a light complexion, light eyes, and strawberry- blonde hair. All through childhood and adolescence, I was the "pale" one, the one who was different. The other kids were all caramel-skinned, dark-eyed, and dark-haired. Their features, I thought, were so beautifully defined. I didn't fit in. The stares seemed for me with several spotlights directed my way. Albeit, adoration was not their motive. Couldn't I just be invisible?

Then there was Josie, the dominant force in our 5th grade class who gleefully attacked anyone she saw as different with her loud mouth and derogatory comments. One time, I was traipsing through the playground when, *Ooh, no... there she was!* Josie was headed straight toward me with a group of kids who were more than eager to follow and watch her in action.

I frantically searched for the nearest escape but ended up directly in her path. She stopped abruptly, paused, and then slowly eyed me up and down. I froze. "What's wrong with you? You don't have any eyebrows and your hair is orange! It's so ugly," she taunted. The laughter I heard would stay with me and become the soundtrack of my life.

Later that night, as I studied my reflection, I could see Josie standing over me spouting those heart-piercing words. My eyes welled up with tears once more. The worst part was that she was right. My frizzy, strawberry-blond hair, fair skin, freckles, no eyebrows, and a pudgy body made me think of Bozo the clown. I figured I could always get a job with the circus, if I ever wanted. I glared at that ugly girl and let my ghostly forehead drop to my freckled forearm. I really was a freak.

Unfortunately, junior high did not bring an improvement, but rather confirmed the miserable truth. Josie was merely a 2 on the Richter scale compared to the junior high kids. Many wanted to beat me up over my looks. Physical abuse too! It would have been better to wear long sleeves and throw a paper bag over my head.

"Don't rub up against her... you'll get white." "I bet they can see you from satellites, cause you glow in the dark, even during the day." These were the taunts from my classmates.

Even the teachers joined in. During a history discussion on WWII, Mr. Jackson talked about the Nazis, Hitler, and the slaughtering of millions of Jews. He pointed at me and announced, "The Aryan race looked like her." My cheeks burned like fire, and again, all eyes were on me. So now my appearance was also responsible for the death of Jewish people!

The wind blew the tears off my cheeks as I walked toward the town center to watch a parade with my parents. "One cotton candy, please." Oh, how I loved the sticky, sweet fluffiness... a temporary escape ball of sugar. I rushed off to the restroom.

"What? No! Come on!" I tugged on that zipper for at least 5 minutes, then snap! It popped off, and I stood there with my crotch exposed, wondering how I was going to cover up. My cropped t-shirt wouldn't do the trick. What could I say? It was the 80's. My mom, I knew, would have a safety pin. I managed to maneuver through the crowds with a paper napkin covering the area. When I finally found my mom, all she could say was, "We're going to have to stop feeding you. You're fat."

The shame trickled through my veins like poison. I went home and told the ugly girl in the mirror, "They want a freak... I'll show them a freak."

First, I used food coloring and dyed my contacts. Then, I painted streaks in my hair with markers. I wore a trash bag as a dress. I could play the role that everyone had designated for me. In fact, if I acted out the part with enough confidence and admitted to the world that I really was weird, inside and out, perhaps feeling accepted would no longer be an issue.

They accepted me all right... the boys, that is. At the time, their compliments seemed sincere, but they were playing to my insecurities. It's amazing how quickly people learn to manipulate and prey on the most vulnerable. Maybe I just wanted to feel pretty, even once, even for a few moments. Never mind that their kindness required me to be physical. I ached for the praise and needed to hear it, even if it was a lie.

I began obsessing over the things I thought I could control. My mama's southern cooking, for example, was so delicious, but not the healthiest. Both my mom and dad were overweight, and I didn't want to end up like them, so I stopped eating. "Oh, I'm going out with friends, so I'll eat with them," or "I already ate at school," and "I'm going to eat this in my room." I invented any excuse possible to avoid consuming calories. I knew I had to eat something, so water, black coffee, celery, and carrots became my daily nourishment. I was only fifteen and downing 10-12 Dexatrim per day. This continued for over a year.

Makeup and pills became true and constant companions. They serviced me beautifully. My eyebrows finally stood out, and my freckles remained hidden. There weren't many options for mousse back then, so I had to buy Afro sheen, but who cares? It tamed the wild beast on top of my head. I even had a boyfriend, Forrest, who seemed to appreciate me for my true self. High school marked a turning point for me; no more misery, as long as I stuck to the plan.

"Tina," snap, snap. "Are you all right?" The blurriness slowly dissipated, and the hard, cold tiles underneath my fragile body startled me a bit. A small group of classmates encircled me, but Forrest was right by my side, smiling at me with one hand holding mine, while the other hand held my head. I fainted 2-3 times per week on average. Switching to Slimfast apparently didn't balance my blood sugar levels, but I could handle the fainting. I could even handle the excruciatingly painful migraines. But when my period disappeared, the real worry set in. Forrest and I were sexually active and certainly not ready to play house.

My parents set up appointment after appointment with every doctor imaginable. They provided my folks with no answers or solutions, because I refused to share any of my secrets. I had made a deal with that ugly girl in the mirror a long time before, and I was not about to dishonor our agreement. I exercised to that damn Jane Fonda video like crazy. The sweat poured out of me as I reached for the ceiling with both arms stiff and straight, then I pulled them back down to my side as I lifted each knee to my chest. "81, 82, 83, 84!..." No giving up now. "You're going to exercise yourself to death!" my mom exclaimed.

If only that were enough; the only opinion I really wanted was Forrest's. I could actually spend time alone with him without wearing much makeup, or smoothing out my hair and covering up my white skin. We walked to the park one day, hand in hand, snapping pictures of nature, people, and anything else that interested us. I was not particularly dolled up, but it didn't really matter.

We approached a wooden bench where I plopped myself down and stared up at the sky, silently asking it about my future. Forrest pointed the camera at me, and I begged him not to take a picture, but he did anyway. "This is totally you." I was afraid to look, and at first glance, I cringed, but then looked again and saw the playful personality that he had captured. I was silly and completely unaware of who I really was, but he valued me the same. "Hey Tina, I want you to stop what you're doing.... You're killing yourself."

The next day in class, I just sat there very still, completely zoned out, repeating his words over and over in my head. "Tina?" My heart skipped a beat as I realized that Ms. Sain was calling me up to her desk. I wasn't in trouble, right? No... a straight-A student like me... no way. I hesitantly walked over to her and tried to slow down my breathing and keep my knees from knocking.

"You know who you remind me of?" she asked.

I shrugged my shoulders and gave her a half smile.

"Lucille Ball," she told me, and I said, "thanks" and then awkwardly returned to my seat.

Lucille Ball? Was it the orange hair we had in common? Lucille Ball? *I Love Lucy*... Ricky Ricardo... Fred and Ethel. All sorts of images flashed through my mind as I recalled the many reruns I'd watched over the years. She really was a phenomenal comedian, entrepreneur, and entertainer. Did Ms. Sain really notice any of Lucille's traits in me? I struggled to accept her sincere compliment.

If that's what she meant then perhaps, just maybe, I was destined to be somebody. When I crawled into bed that night, I retraced the picture Forrest took of me and began to recognize something else. I definitely possessed a look unlike any other. But could I actually see beauty in my vulnerability?

I met with one more doctor, and this time, something clicked. After asking some questions and doing a quick examination, he gave us his suggestions. I sincerely hoped that he wouldn't announce to my parents that I had an eating disorder. He never uttered those words, but I can only presume he knew the truth for he suggested a nutrition plan. It ended up being a gift. There were so many meal options to choose from that I felt like I hadn't lost any control, but gained a healthy perspective on food. I actually bought a wok and started cooking for my family.

Thank God I... ® *Am an Empowered Woman:*

Once I realized that I could achieve my goals in a healthy way, the need to sabotage myself eventually dissolved. I was proud to have turned my life around and have a positive effect on both my parents' lifestyles. Unfortunately, both of them had left this world by the time that I was twenty-five. But as much as I grieved for them, their passing forced me to grow up. My mom and dad had been my driving force. When they died, I realized I could feel good for myself and not do things just to seek approval. The universe created a perfect balance so that even though I was losing, I was also gaining.

To this day, I still color in my eyebrows, but who cares? That's why makeup was created. The point is that I've accepted my strengths and weaknesses and can see the perfection in all of it. It took a few minutes to reach this level of thinking, but the switch finally turned on, once certain teachers and high school sweethearts put me in my place.

I'm not surprised I became a comedian, a woman who loves photo shoots, an entrepreneur, an author, a TV personality, and a mother as well. They used to stare at me as a kid... they might as well keep on starin'. Now, when I look in the mirror, I see a woman on a mission who can go out in public without any makeup — and a beautiful woman at that. Thank you, Lucy, for paving the way for us "Gingers" and bringing me back to life.

The applause begins, the spotlight focuses in, and the announcer roars, "AND NOW... TINA MARIE JONES!"

♥♥♥

In the business of teaching, coaching, and consulting since 1999, three time best-selling author, internationally recognized inspirational speaker, radio/television talk show host, and Certified Life Coach, Tina Marie Jones has made a true name for herself in teaching the importance of self-esteem and how it affects our overall health, happiness, and success. Her messages are fun and easy to digest and in the end, empower her audiences to make positive changes that last a lifetime. People all over the world seek out Tina Marie to take their careers, lives and dreams to the next level. Through her coaching, clients learn how to navigate difficult conversations, choices, and pathways in their lives with ease, grace, and playful curiosity.

Your Journey to Self-Discovery
By Lisa Christine Christiansen

There's an old adage that says the journey of a thousand miles begins with a single footstep. Today, I'd like you to take that initial step with me on the journey of your personal empowerment. Start by grabbing a mirror. Now, I would like everyone to hold up the mirror and on a piece of paper write down what you see? Who is that person in the reflection?

The image in the mirror is only a reflection of you but even so it is one of the most powerful images one can see. Who are you? Looking at this mirror and really observing the image is the most important thing you will take away from what I am sharing with you now as we begin your journey to personal empowerment.

I have prayed for only one person and each of you is that one person. Despite all the messages we get bombarded with on television, in fashion magazines and even from that annoying little inner voice, the person you are looking at in the mirror is special. You are enough. Not only are you one of a kind, but also by going on this journey with me you will see that by being the best version of you is truly powerful. You are beautiful. You are strong.

As you accept your authentic self and allow your inner beauty to be reflected I thank you for being that one person God intends for you to be. As you read this please understand that we are now a team of one.

Now you can understand we have disproved Einstein's theory that the number one is the loneliest number. One in this sense is anything but lonely. From this day forward always remember if you find yourself by yourself, which is going to happen to all of us, you are not alone. You are not alone because all that you need is within you. Think about the reflection of the person you observed in the mirror. Think about the strengths and special characteristics you wrote down as you looked at the reflection in the mirror.

Now and forever have faith in yourself when it comes to making a decision. Listen to that inner voice and trust yourself. Are you the person driving a car in the rain that waits until they see two or three other cars with their windshield wipers on to know that it is okay to turn theirs on? If so now is the time for a change, be confident in the individual you are and be the leader.

I would like you to take a piece of paper and write who the most important relationship you've ever had in your life with is? Take a moment and reflect on this question. This doesn't mean that there is a right or wrong answer in the traditional sense. The "right" answer is your answer. By that I mean what's important to you. Just think about the person that is or was the one that you have the most significant relationship with today and right it down.

Everyone who wrote down "me" give yourself a round of applause, If your wrote anything else beginning now commit to take a moment out of your day to make yourself a priority because you are the only one who can decide what you are worth it is only then that others will appreciate your value.

Although there really isn't a wrong answer, the healthiest answer is "you". The most important relationship we will ever have is the one we have with ourselves. Until we can be honest with ourselves, accepting our imperfections which make us perfect, appreciating our dreams, embracing our fears and all the battle scars we've acquired along our life's journey, how can anyone else accept us? How can anyone value you if you don't value yourself?

We teach others how to treat us... remember we can't give what we don't have. As unique as we all are one thing we share in common is we often find ourselves emotionally drained from giving and nurturing others in the many roles we find ourselves in which is a beautiful gift. That amazing child within you reflected in the mirror is special and deserves to be nurtured too. By allowing yourself to be important in your life you allow yourself to be a better spouse, a better parent, a better child, and a better friend. You have the emotional constitution to stay in the moment. When you give yourself permission to dream the impossible incredible things happens.

Always remember that information linked to emotion is retained. In life eighty percent is psychology and the other twenty percent are the mechanics. A person who knows where she is going will figure out ways to overcome the challenges along the way. As you walk along your personal journey of personal empowerment you will have moments, days and perhaps even periods of life in which you will be confronted with frustration. When you are feeling frustrated and overwhelmed, get excited! Frustration only means you are about to have a breakthrough. Likewise confusion also means you are about to learn something, stay excited.

By learning something as you grow from the frustration and confusion you encounter remember that you are developing character and internal wealth. Internal wealth is another way to perceive wisdom. The internal wealth and wisdom that you acquire as you walk down your life's path is what you can give and share with others who come behind you. It is always helpful sharing a concern or struggle with another individual who has experienced it and found a way to break through it. This wealth starts in the mind and in the heart.

Regardless of what your outcome is, pick someone to emulate. Look at the individuals who have found ways to succeed in the areas you are interested in now. Find someone who has a similar passion. Be brave, step up and ask for guidance. Seek a mentor and invest in that relationship. After all, we are the five people we surround ourselves with. Think about that for a moment and decide if those five people are helping you grow or keeping you stuck. Once you answer that question, take action.

Define where you are. Determine what can be done in a day, a week and a month to move you further a long your journey to reach the outcome you identified for yourself. Write your outcome in detail. Write your outcome in lots of places so that you will focus on it. Our daily focus either moves us toward or away from our outcome so be proactive. Because the most important relationship you have with another person is the relationship you have with that amazing person in the mirror, make it a priority to focus on your outcome daily. One way in which you can accomplish this is to set your outcome is if it is already happened. There's a nugget of truth in that old saying fake it until you make it. "Act as if until" you have already achieved your outcome or as if you are currently living it.

Keep your focus. Success is the only option that is acceptable. Set another outcome as soon as your goal is met. Always take your outcome and make it manageable by dividing it into bite size pieces.

Love like you've never been hurt. Keep in mind that the angrier you get the more static in your brain. The more static in your brain the less you can hear what's being said to you.

Thank God I... ® *Am an Empowered Woman:*

Thus, so remember to live and love as love truly conquers all. May the love you have hidden deep within your heart find its way to the love in your dreams. Make the laughter that you find in your tomorrow wipe away the pain you find in your yesterdays.

Staying in love is a decision. Loving and valuing yourself is also a decision and it's not always easy. Anger, tears and laughter are all expected and okay in an interpersonal relationship. Through it all trust that you are truly in love. When you love yourself you have an abundance of love. Remember, love is a gift that you give without expectation of its return. It is then that your true love shines through and that is when you really know that what is inside of you, your inner wealth, your inner wisdom, and inner love is all that you need. The good news is that all of those gifts are already within you.

By learning to love myself and recognize the gifts that are within me, I am confident and secure enough to encourage you to step out in faith by looking at the woman you are today, seeing where you are and deciding where you want to be.

Because I am walking my own journey of self-discovery I can tell you that yes, you'll get frustrated and confused and those are all good things. I can't say I always knew the woman I saw in the mirror what I can say is I have always appreciated this woman and her unique abilities because of the mentors that I have been blessed to have walk in front of me and beside me, I am the woman that I am today because of you.

For those of you who know me from thank God I... Volume 3, I would like to take this opportunity to thank you with my deepest gratitude for allowing me to share my challenges that I encountered on my journey to personal empowerment. Thank you for accepting me for who I am. I have a long road ahead of me and that's exciting. Now as I walk victoriously, I encourage you to walk beside me through my own personal awakening. Today I come to you with the opportunity to share with you my appreciation and love for you.

What has my journey taught me so far? From the seeds of necessity grows success. From the sweat of desperation come the seeds of purpose. Let's have some fun as we grow together walking along our path recognizing that we're never really alone, that we have all of the skills we need to get us through today within us. Trust that whatever tomorrow brings will be okay because you have the skills and tools from your own inner wealth, wisdom and love to make it.

Everyone has a primary question, what is yours? Mine is "what action will I take today to create the tomorrow I am committed to living". Equally as important, how can you create a destination that will allow you to be authentic to the complex, talented and ever growing gift that you are? Live in strength by making the situations you experience on your journey of personal empowerment into opportunities to serve others and yourself.

Creator of extraordinary lives, Lisa Christiansen has impacted the lives of millions of people from 30 countries. A recognized authority on the psychology of leadership, organizational turnaround, and peak performance, Lisa's strategies for achieving lasting results and fulfillment are currently regarded as a platinum standard in the coaching industry. As a result, she has served as an advisor to leaders around the world for the last two decades, including Heads of State and the U.S. Army. Christiansen has also consulted with Olympic athletes such as Dara Torres, world-renowned musicians like members of the rock band Journey and pop superstar Kelly Clarkson, as well as Fortune 500 CEOs, other psychologists, and world-class entertainers.

Thank God I Can Create Miracles
By Alida Fehily

One night I was scrolling through *The Secret* website and reading about the different teachers. Suddenly my phone rang and — amazingly — as I picked it up, the person on the line asked me, 'What is the secret?'

I started to laugh because I knew that it was a reflection of my own thoughts. After the call, I continued searching through the site and I came across an image of Jack Canfield, co-author of the *Chicken Soup for the Soul* books. In a fleeting glance, I saw him wink at me!! I knew that this was a divine message and straight away I interpreted it as: 'Green light. Go ahead. Start writing!' That was the day I first started to create the WIZ-cARDs™.

Because of the universal message I had received, I knew I had to create something that would reflect my reality as a universal message. I like to use the term 'The Law of Reflection' because I believe everything you experience in life is merely reflecting your own reality.

As I was creating the WIZ-cARDs™, I resonated with each and every one of the cards until I saw something in my own reality that had manifested:

My imagination creates miracles... What miracles can you imagine?

Break through limitations — go beyond what you think is possible. Keep your faith; your dreams will unfold. If you've thought it, go past the fear and live it. Your imagination is the start of creation, so be open to what is on its way. Dream big — it's your guide to your destiny. Only you have the power to change your reality. Imagine seeing your world through different eyes... Now create your life. *My imagination creates miracles, etc.*

The cards took quite some time to develop. Once I was ready to have the WIZ-cARDs™ printed I began to encounter problem after problem. I had a publisher who resized the cards for his own fiscal benefit, not mine. I wasted nearly one year of my time with his mucking around until I finally cancelled the deal with him.

As I started to gather testimonials, there was one particularly well-known writer who agreed to give me one. I sent her the eBook and waited, and waited, and never heard back. This became just another hold-up in an already lengthy and at-times frustrating process.

The question: "Is this really going to happen?" kept popping up in my mind, were these cards destined to be made at all, I wondered. But deep within I knew that what you most aspire to is your divine purpose in life. In the midst of creating these cards, I was fulfilling my dreams. Through this my life was meaningful and inspiring.

One Sunday morning, as I was sitting in the kitchen, the sun shining through the window, I opened my weekly horoscope and it read, 'Dear Aries, what you are missing is right under your nose'. I sat there staring into space thinking, "What have I missed?" I really couldn't think of anything.

During the course of the day I was sent three emails regarding Jack Canfield. Now I know that when the universe presents something three times, you should pay attention to the message! I got up and walked outside into the garden. All of a sudden, I felt like a hot bolt of lightning shot through me. What did I miss? It was Jack Canfield's testimonial that I needed. That old universal message I received with a wink came rushing back to me. I would not have even created the WIZ-cARDs™ if it weren't for Jack.

I couldn't get to my laptop quick enough to email a friend to ask him if he would pass my eBook onto Jack. I was overwhelmed with excitement; I knew that his testimonial was coming through. Now I had to write Jack a letter. Hmm... I wondered what I was going to say to him, that he winked at me? I figured he'd either say I was some weirdo nutcase or he would love it. The important thing, I decided, was that I wrote from my heart and explained my experience to him, and how he had inspired me to create the dream in my heart. So that's just what I told him.

Over the following week I put all of my power into manifesting Jack's testimonial, affirming to myself, opening my heart to love. The inspiration I was feeling was like a driving force. I had a clear mind and had let go of any limiting beliefs. I sent the graphic artist an email to say I had one last change, that I was getting a testimonial from Jack. When I went to bed at night I tossed and turned with the excitement that I had everything in the bag, so to speak.

After a week I dropped the thought of having the testimonial. My ego wanted it and wanted it right now, but there were obstacles beyond my comprehension. I woke up one morning without a thought in my mind at all about the cards or the testimonial. I turned on my laptop and went into to my email and there it was: an email from Jack Canfield. I could feel my heart start to pound when I saw the email from the man himself. When the universe provides it truly carries with it a *wow* factor that is challenging to describe yet you know it when you feel it. This confirmed that my mind was in sync with the dream in my heart, and my manifestation was in alignment with the universe.

The WIZ-cARDs™ were four years in the making. Even with all the delays and problems, I kept persevering. I became quite obsessed with my purpose in life; I knew I had created these cards for a reason. Though I wondered why it took so long. There also needed to be time in order for me to befriend Jack's friend and eventually obtain Jack's testimonial. I knew then that it was the perfect time for printing. This was an amazing lesson to learn: to let go of expectations on things manifesting a certain way. Everything is created in divine timing, perfection and order.

Thank God I... allowed my intuition to uncover the information I required; I am guided by this in my own life, and it allows me to assess other people's feelings, motives, desires – to tap into their space and help them create and make profound decisions in their own lives.

I have devoted myself to empowering people to live their lives free of stress and heartache, as well as encouraging them to discover the truth that is otherwise hidden in darkness. It's essential to follow your dreams and no matter how long it takes, never give up. Life is a journey, not a destination. If you can imagine it, you can create it!

Alida Fehily is an International Wisdom Consultant, Australian Psychics Association award-winning "Psychic of the Year (WA) 2005", a Demartini Method Trained Facilitator, an intuitive healer, and author of the WIZ-cARDs®, which are a wonderful tool to help people find the pathway within and to discover your own reality. WIZ-cARDs® could help create the life of your dreams and inspire you to live according to your highest potential.

Alida has helped thousands of people see their futures more vividly and clearly through face-to-face consultations, public speaking, radio talks, workshops, and internet social media. She consults with people from all walks of life, including business owners, celebrities, and entrepreneurs. She doesn't need a magic wand; she just is magic! Visit her at <u>AlidaFehily.com</u>

Thank God For My Divorce
By Dr. Dena Churchill

Your first thought would probably not be thank God for my struggles and challenges.

Once you have the courage to even say the word DIVORCE... you may cry. Then you may begin your journey into the scary unknown with fears and emotions in high gear. The first step is always the hardest... to admit this first to yourself, and then to tell someone else.

At this time my life feels as though it has been put into a blender. My clinic, custody of our children, and our family home is put on the table for the courts and lawyers to dice, dissect and decide our fate. I almost wish my spouse had made the final decision because now I live not only with the grief of loss and the fear of the consequences, but guilt of "destroying our family."

As I lay in a cold bed, my heart is racing, my mind jumps from one thought to another, and my stomach is burning with fear. I am clinging to the edge of our bed, in a fetal position, tasting my salty tears as they wet the pillow under my cheek, trying to swallow the lump in my throat. I told my spouse tonight that I want a divorce but I am not sure where to go next. What about the kids? Where will I live? Maybe things will change? At this stage in my life, will I find another partner? Am I making a mistake? What have I done?

I did this oscillation for a time, as we all do when our string has been plucked. First, I wanted the divorce, then him, then me. My mind felt like a plate of assorted biscuits. How was I possibly going to get through this? First I had to see how it would serve him to have me leave. As I was empowering myself I worried for him. Once I could see the benefits of empowerment and opportunity for both of us in the divorce, the oscillations stopped, my vision was clear, and I had the confidence to move on. The challenge of the divorce would empower our family to greater heights of strength, confidence, and love.

It feels as though I am on a battlefield being cornered on all sides. I have pulled my children, my parents, and my spouse on the field with me. My parents invested in my business, which employs my mother; so this decision to get a divorce affects my entire family. My fears are fueled about life and safety, as the police officers advised me to change the locks on the doors to my home. "Dear God, please sustain our lives, helping me get through this divorce with love and grace. Show me the way."

Dr. John Demartini has developed a tool called the Demartini Method for dissolving the emotion around the process of letting go. At the onset of my pending separation, I called Dr. Demartini with the question of how to get through a divorce with love and gratitude, thinking that there would be a magic phrase, recommendation, or solution. It took me months to find this but the answers were in me all along.

Initially, I was asked to list the qualities I disliked about my former spouse... this one could have gone on forever. But the list of what I liked was very short. In fact, I could initially only think of two things that I liked about him: that he loaded the dishwasher in a space conserving way and that he shined his shoes well. With a lot of sweat and tears, I eventually pulled out a few more to fill up the page.

Thank God I... ® *Am an Empowered Woman:*

Then as part of this process I was asked to find all these traits I despised in him, in me. Now this was the hardest part for me to do. I am not him. I am the opposite of him (which evidently I have discovered is why the universe put us together). I am not an angry person, I am not aggressive, I am not resentful, and the "I am nots" continued as I resisted seeing myself as a reflection of him.

Some may be stingy with their money and some may be stingy with their sex, but we are all stingy is some capacity. I did get angry and as a Chiropractor, many days aggressive in my treatments. I have been verbally abusive with a telemarketer, or with the publicist that tried to tell me how I should write my press release. I did lie occasionally to the dental hygienist about how often I floss or to my children about that round red Christmas character; I did lie about how many lovers I had or to the telemarketing survey people.

The sobering result is to see this reflection and that I was everything to the same degree (maybe in a different capacity) that I was accusing him of being. The traits that I was denying most in myself were the ones in him about which I was most critical.

The next part of this process was to see that other people would describe my former spouse in the exact opposite way. His family and friends, our neighbors, and his coworkers and staff would describe him differently, and there would be others equal in magnitude that would describe me differently depending on who was on the other end of the phone line. At this point in the seminar, I am feeling my body relax but there is a lump appearing in my throat as I am literally trying to swallow the fact that what I had believed as truths were really my own labels and judgments seen through my limited perspective. Now naturally those that share my values will agree with me and those that share his will agree with him. Life is your perception and the color of the picture depends on which glasses you are wearing.

A third component of this method is for me to see how the traits I have labeled negative have a benefit and how the positive traits can actually do a disservice. How can yelling at someone be beneficial? How does lying serve us? At this moment, I am looking at the door and wondering if I can slip out without anyone noticing because I can't see this being useful. It is actually quite aggravating to have my beliefs and thoughts questioned. Dare I say it, but I am beginning to resent this Demartini dude. He doesn't know my husband, and how can he be asking me to see the benefit in something that everyone knows is disgraceful behavior.

I am starting to imagine myself walking up to the seminar "guru," tossing the book in his lap, and storming out. I don't care what anyone else thinks; they don't know my husband and what he is like. I'm almost committed to leaving. Back and forth my thoughts are racing on either side of the exit. I move a little further in my mind into the future to imagine what I will feel like after I leave. Will I still be angry? Yes, likely even more angry now, because I have paid $1000 in advance for this seminar and have not found the "a-ha" moment I was hoping to experience! My desire to release my own anger, not lose the money I had invested in this process, and the fear of John Demartini embarrassing me kept me glued to my seat.

My head, at this moment, is feeling like a plate of crushed assorted biscuits, and the crumbs settling into my eyes and ears are clouding my senses. In between reciting a number of swear words to myself, I kept looking for the answer. Struggling through the workbook, doubting the process, and fighting the method, I found some grace in this one phrase: Dr. Demartini questioned, "If challenge makes us stronger and support only sustains us, which is more loving, challenge or support?" As I scanned the past memories of all the events I had labeled challenging they did indeed bring growth in strength, confidence and resourcefulness that otherwise I would not have experienced. Maybe there is something relieving in this message. Could it be that love is both the support and the challenge?

The last nail that cracked the cage around my heart was that if my former spouse were to act in the exact opposite way, I wouldn't like this any better. When you finally get this realization, you comprehend that all is perfect just as it is, that only through his challenge and him being him, I am me.

I criticized my husband for not being spiritual and not contributing to my spiritual journey. He would not attend church, nor participate in dinner graces, and labeled himself as an atheist. One morning after mediating on this to understand how this could be a service, I broke into tears. I fell to my knees at the side of my bed uncontrollably sobbing as I'd clearly seen this as the grace of God guiding my path through him. His stories of "after death" experiences would not have been near as powerful had he been attached to one particular religious faith. It was this knowing and understanding that began to shake my belief in organized religion into true spirituality — the knowing that lives in the heart of the universe.

There are no broken families, but families that are dynamically changing and growing into different forms. The marriage relationship has transformed to a divorce relationship to a former spouse relationship. There are two homes instead of one, and you could say that we have just diversified the family assets for our children. There will be new supports and challenges in the next form as it is neither better nor worse but growing in new lessons of love.

As I am learning to love all parts of me — the builder and the destroyer, the kind and the unkind, the peaceful and the warring — I see my former spouse as one of my greatest teachers in or out of the marriage.

His challenging and questioning of my purpose was to test my commitment. Even the shared custody arrangement that initially tore my heart in two was a gift that gave the boys a father that was dedicated to them with purpose and presence. The free time without the children opened the door for me to follow the second part of my purpose in writing and speaking to the hearts and souls of others.

Dr. Dena Churchill is an international speaker, author, and world innovator of women's empowerment in health and wellness. She is known for her ability to deeply connect with audiences through clarity, wisdom, and humor to help you "Envision and Achieve Your Best", unleashing the power of the authentic you! DrDenaChurchill.com

Thank God I Have Faith
By Susie Young-Tatum

"Be strong." My mother's words pierced every cell of my body that morning and continue to resonate with me to this day. Her tone was strong and yet somehow it still relayed the underlying heartbreak of what she was about to tell me. I knew in that moment that a door had closed behind me. Despite her command, no amount of strength could ever open it again.

Behind that door had been the simple, complete, and relatively sheltered life of the small Nebraska farming community where I grew up. It was a place where everyone knew each other, perhaps even a little too well. However, this familiarity only led to caring.

Every evening in our small town, the six o'clock whistle blew, alerting the end of the day. Dad would arrive home, giving mom their traditional three kisses as she stood over the stove cooking dinner. My sister and I would then begin our ritual of grabbing his legs, and he'd give us a ride through the kitchen to the bathroom where he would then wash up for the evening.

Dad was a gentle, kind, and loving man. He was a tall man with a physically fit frame. Dark hair and big, green eyes radiated humility, honesty, and strength.

At the ages of three and four, my sister and I were only dimly aware of what Dad really did with his days. We were just glad he was home as we stomped from room to room, each wearing one of the work boots he had carefully left by the back door.

But as I raced toward adulthood, I began to understand with great pride who my father really was. By then, Dad had built half the homes in our small town — homes that only had their doors locked when the carnival came to town. He was respected everywhere, as both a businessman and a carpenter. People waited for months to entrust Kenny with building their most valuable possession.

"George called again. He's wondering if the house plans are finished. He's excited that you're almost done with Campbell's home," Mom said.

"After that I'm hanging doors at Schmidt's and then it's George's turn," Dad chuckled. "I'll give him a call."

Despite his busy schedule, Dad found time to coach my softball team, take me to band lessons early in the morning, and attend all of my volleyball and cheerleading events. One day, he announced that he had bought land next to the railroad tracks. He had a dream. "I'm going to build a trailer court. A safe, affordable place for 30 families to live," he said. "Want to go to the trailer court with me?" he'd ask. "I need to turn the sprinklers on and mow the grass."

I'd hop in the baby blue Dodge pickup that always smelled like vinyl. Peppermint candies and a pipe filled with cherry blend tobacco lay in the ashtray. He'd drive down the winding gravel road that led to rows of well-kept trailers, exchanging waves with each car that passed. People would be sitting on lawn chairs in front of their homes, enjoying the evening. Dad loved his "little community."

In college, I felt inspired to start a Bible study in my sorority house. Dad was proud of me for that. I'd often ask him for advice on questions that came up. One girl asked me about her grandfather who had committed suicide. Could he be in Heaven? "Only God knows that man's heart," Dad stated firmly and without judgment.

About this time, Dad developed a virus in his eye similar to shingles. His faith was strong, but the pain increased. This made it difficult for him to drive, go to church, or even walk outside in the sunlight. He traveled to see specialists, but nothing they gave him seemed to relieve the pain. He tried doing his daily work of carpentry and taking care of his rental properties and trailer court. One night, my junior year, I received the news that my dad had been at the trailer court checking on a young boy and his family as they had just become tenants. After being at the trailer court, Dad drove down the familiar road and crossed the tracks on his way to visit another family. "Susie, your dad has been in a car accident. He's been hit by a train."

As I hurried to the hospital, there was one thing that kept me from losing it. I prayed. As horrible as it was, I kept thinking he didn't look as bad as I'd expected. The next morning, Dad had a six-hour surgery that removed a small part of his brain. "He is lucky to be alive," the surgeon said.

Dad lay helpless. Chained to his hospital bed so he couldn't touch his head wounds. A couple days later he was tenaciously walking the halls of the hospital. Within a week he was back home with broken ribs and bandaged head, lying in a hospital-style bed in the basement family room. At forty-five, my dad still had a lot of life to live. It would take time, but I was sure God had a plan.

In a month, I was home for Christmas break and watched in dismay as he desperately tried to get out of bed on his own to read Christmas cards from people all over the state. Tears welled up in his eyes at the immense outpouring of love. The support was overwhelming.

After the break, I jumped back into my studies. Cheerleading tryouts were in March with a two-week "boot camp" before going in front of a panel of judges. I called home for my saddle shoes.

"Hi, Dad. How are you feeling?" I asked.

"Oh, I'm doing OK. How are you?"

"I need my saddle shoes for tryouts. Can you send them?"

"Yes, we can," he said.

A couple days later, I was awoken by a call from my mother. I wondered why she would be calling me at such an early hour of the morning.

"Susie, I need you to BE STRONG. Your dad has shot himself."

I was told a piercing wail came out of me. Was I dreaming? What had just happened? Why?

Fifty miles from home I saw an ambulance pass in the other direction. On the drive back, my brother and I pulled over and called home. Was it Dad in the ambulance? It wasn't. He had died before we could make it home.

Shock is the only emotion to describe the next several days.

When I arrived, the house was swarming with people. Friends and relatives had come from across the country. Days later during the funeral, the church was so full that they had to set up seating in the basement so people could listen to the service through speakers. Others lined up outside the front doors and down the church steps. They had all come to honor the carpenter, a humble man who had impacted so many in just the simple way he lived his life.

It was a cold and rainy morning; I imagined God was crying, His tears flowing from Heaven. But then, why would my all-powerful God be crying? How could He let my father die?

My faith was challenged with confusion and immense pain that I felt. I went back to school not knowing how I would go on. Somehow, I found myself wandering from class to class. I remember reflecting that life was beautiful. In my awareness of dad's life-and-death battle, I discovered how precious and delicate life was. It seemed so strange that life was just... somehow... continuing.

How could Dad really be gone when he had done so much to help others realize their dreams? And then, two thoughts hit me, one right after the other. One was that Dad wasn't really gone — not completely. He was in the laughter of the children he cared about in the trailer court. He was in the families' homes that he built. He was here in the glistening drops of rain as I walked across campus.

The other thought was, in fact, that as his daughter, I was standing in the middle of one of his dreams. Dad's dream had been to raise a family, to contribute to his community, and to leave something of value behind. He had contributed; my sister, brother, and I were people with loving hearts and good strong values. It was clear that Dad had accomplished his dream. And in fact, I was a part of his legacy in the world; I was part of him that was still alive.

Back at school with a new sense of purpose, I opened up to my friends about my faith. I wrote Bible verses and positive quotes, and placed them throughout the sorority house. I allowed God to be in control. I knew I would never fully know the reason Dad committed suicide, and that was OK. That was faith.

I began to lead the cheerleading squad in prayer before the games and continued to lead the Bible study in the sorority house. I was also teaching small children in Sunday school while mentoring others in their faith. Many people who were in my life at that time went on to lead amazing lives of charity and have Christian leadership roles. One woman, who committed her life to Christ at the sorority Bible study, today helps her husband in one of the world's largest charity organizations. One friend became a Pastor and ministers to people through his counseling. Another manages a Christian camp for youth. The list goes on.

Through faith, I picked myself up, dusted myself off, and kept going while giving thanks for the JOY during a very tragic time in my life. I got through it, knowing there is a plan far greater than I will ever understand. I am empowered not by my own doing, but by God.

The saying, "actions speak louder than words" is so true. I didn't set out to change people's idea of how to cope with loss; it was faith that led my actions. I learned life is about the journey. It's about rejoicing in the good times, staying thankful in the bad times, and knowing life is about experiencing both. The joy comes from knowing that I got through it by the grace of God. Thank God I have Faith.

After college, Susie Young-Tatum worked as a successful businesswoman, a broker, and eventually moved to Chicago. She became a Vice President of a large corporation by the time she was 27. She now owns her own business, helping to feed children in Third World Countries and helping others with their health and wholeness. She is a Coach and mentor, with an emphasis on leadership, wellness, and finances. She is the mother of two beautiful daughters. Susie aspires to be the best she can be, and to help others to do the same with their lives.

Thank God I Was Diagnosed With Diabetes
By Wanda Muir-Oliver

It was a beautiful day Tuesday, April 09, 2011. I was excited about attending The Baltimore Times Newspaper 25th Anniversary and helping the Founder Jay Bramble (CEO) celebrate her success. I had already RSVP'd for the event some time ago and informed several friends that I would be attending the event. I also was looking forward to hearing and meeting the keynote speaker Daymond John (CEO of FUBU) for the event.

I had a snack to eat and a big glass of orange juice. However, I had been feeling ill, and when it was near time to attend the event, I still felt sick, and physically drained. The first idea that entered my mind was that one of the Autistic children that I worked with perhaps gave me the 24-hour virus. I had never felt this sick before. I began to pray and asked God to heal my body. I also asked him to grant me a long life to spend time with family and friends and live life to the fullest.

I sat in my chair in the living room resting for a while hoping I would be feeling better in time. I was determined to go to the event so I got up from my chair and walked outside to my car. I put my key into the ignition and turned it, the car would not start. I had no problem with the car before. I tried starting the car many times without success. I said to myself, I guess it was not meant for me to go to the event. Since I have gotten older, I have taught myself not to worry about things that you have no control over. I thought of calling a cab, but when I looked at the time, an hour of the program had already begun.

Thank God I... ® *Am an Empowered Woman:*

After no success with transportation getting me to the Ms. Bramble event, I went back into the house and went to bed. I woke up the next morning still not feeling well. I said a prayer and got a ride to work, anyway. However, on Friday morning I did not get up; I laid in bed feeling really bad. I telephoned my doctor to see if I could make an appointment to fit me in his schedule. Dr. Charles Moore said, "sure, you can come in at 4 pm today." I continued to lay in bed until it was near time to wash and dress and head out the door for my doctor's appointment. When getting into my car to drive to the doctor's office, I did not believe that I would make it there; I felt so ill. My eyes became blurry, several times en route to the doctor's office. I pulled my car over on the side of the road and prayed.

Finally, I arrived at the doctor's office, walked in, and signed in at the desk and was asked by the receptionist to have a seat please in the waiting area. She said, "The doctor will see you soon."

The doctor had a half full house, almost every seat in the waiting area occupied by others waiting to see him. I went over to the receptionist and informed her that I could not sit down. I expressed that I felt horrible and it felt like I was going to pass out. The receptionist went into the doctor's examination room and informed him of my issue. The receptionist came back into the waiting area and said to me, "Please come back into the examination room, the doctor will see you shortly."

A few minutes later, the doctor approached me, said hello, and immediately I knew something was wrong with me because I was not joking, laughing, or smiling, like I normally do when I visit his office. The doctor said to me, "You are really sick!" The doctor questioned me and asked me what my symptoms were from feeling ill.

I informed the doctor that I was urinating a lot, tired, and physically drained. The doctor stated that he was going to test my glucose level. After the doctor performed the test, he said, "It's a miracle that you are standing." He stated that I could have blacked out by driving, killing myself or someone else, fallen out, had a major stroke or went into a diabetic coma. The doctor said, "Your glucose reading is at 500." Well, this was Greek to me, I had no idea what that meant. The doctor explained to me that the high glucose level for someone whom is not diabetic is 120. The doctor diagnosed me as being type 2 diabetic; I was devastated.

The lights went out in the entire facility, It was dark. The doctor had to cancel his appointments with the other patients. We found out later that there was an accident that caused the power outage in the area. The doctor resorted to finding a flashlight and working in the dark with me. He indicated that he was going to send me to the hospital. I informed the doctor that I did not wish to go to the hospital.

The doctor and his assistant took my blood pressure and the doctor gave me a shot of insulin and informed me that he needed to bring my glucose down to a lower level. My glucose came down to approximately 350, but he was not satisfied. He said, "It is still way too high." The doctor provided me with a pamphlet on the various foods that I needed to eat and foods not to eat. He also provided me with a prescription, medication, a monitor (glucose reading), some strips, and instructed me how to check my glucose after every meal.

I am grateful to have a wonderful physician. He went over and above the call of duty, treating me beyond his office hours and following up to see how I was progressing every day and scheduling me to come back for a checkup within a week. Whenever I visit my doctor, he takes his time with me, asking me questions and providing me with the latest medical terms. My doctor informs me of my readings from various tests. For instance, my ALC, which lets me know how my body is handling the glucose, also when my blood pressure is taken that it registers in the proper range. In addition my cardiogram test is used to check for preventive measures of a possible stroke, cholesterol levels and if I need to make adjustments to my diet or other factors that I need to know about.

Since my diagnosis of type 2 diabetes, I am informing others about the disease so that they can be proactive in using preventive measures against getting the disease. The American Diabetes Association defines Type 2 diabetes as resulting from a combination of resistance to the action of insulin and insufficient insulin production. Also the 2011 National Diabetes Fact sheet showed that a total of 25.8 million children and adults have diabetes in the United States — 8.3% of the population.

Now I am enjoying myself with lots of exercise, horseback riding, skiing, roller-skating, and walking with my granddaughter, whom is in kindergarten. She is so educated beyond her years. When we go out to eat, she will say, "Mum Mum, you cannot eat that white rice." "Are you buying baked fish, brown rice, and broccoli?" She is emulating her mom, whom she hears saying the same thing when I visit their home. When a meal with dessert is being cooked, she knows that I am unable to eat it. I am grateful that my daughter and granddaughter care and love me so much and would like for me to stay healthy and live a long life; it really helps to give me the incentive to stay on track and do the right thing.

I began wondering how different my life could have been had I not gone to the doctor — would I have been able to do the simple things in life or would I be depending on someone else to help take care of me with a critical illness. I believe that you cannot take life for granted. You have to be thankful every day that you are given life. Now I am living a more purposeful life, helping others as an advocate to eat nutritional foods, exercise, and most importantly, carrying God in your spirit and realizing that he gives you the strength and guides our steps.

Wanda Muir-Oliver is a self-published author, a freelance writer and the author of a poetry book entitled, "Realities of Life"™ with a foreword by Dorothy Irene Height. She is also a contributing author to other literary works, a writer of music, an actress, painter, an activist, motivational speaker and advocate for the homeless. She will introduce a new book of poetry in 2013 and a novel coming in 2014. Wanda is currently writing her screenplay, which is projected to debut in 2014.

web-site:www.Wanda Muir Oliver.com
e-mail: marrshollywood@yahoo.com

Thank God My Daughter Committed Suicide
By Jenetta Barry

There were several occasions after Jenny, my daughter, committed suicide where I contemplated killing myself. It was on the eve of the second anniversary of her death that I succumbed to a very dark moment in my life, when I came seriously close to seeing these thoughts through.

I had traveled to the UK with the intent to set up a light base there, from which to also conduct my business. As the dates for what would have been Jenny's 18th birthday, as well as the second anniversary of her death, drew closer and the winter began to close in. I slipped into my deepest and darkest place. I had organized to take a week off from working in order to visit my brother in Oxford, and some days beforehand, I found myself seriously preparing how to end my life.

As I planned this process through, I began to deeply understand the similarity between physical and emotional pain.

Several years previously, whilst undergoing radiation treatment for cancer, I had hemorrhaged in the intestine; I remember getting to the point where the combination of pain and feeling seriously ill became too overwhelming to handle. It felt as though dying and being released from the pain was the only reasonable option.

Now with these circumstances, I was operating with the same pain, but on an emotional level. An emotional pain that was too overwhelming to cope with. I then realized that I might have an idea of the depth of emotional pain Jen, my daughter, must have felt for most of her life.

"You've fucked up my life! You've fucked up my friendships!"

Jen's words rang in my ears as she stormed out to her bedroom situated on the other side of our house's inner courtyard. We had had an enormous argument, and I, as her Mom, had applied tough love to my 16-year old child.

Over a period of time, Jen had become more and more manipulative. Using the threat of not coping with life and suicide in order to maneuver herself out of being responsible and accountable. This had resulted in her balking at standard house rules required for her safekeeping. I had written her a loving, but firm, letter earlier in the day, indicating to her that challenging and breaking these rules was inappropriate and that it was vital for her well-being that she should conform. This had resulted in our argument and now she was in her room packing her bags to leave home.

I attempted to distract myself by sending a cell phone text to a friend but finally with a feeling of immense unease, I went to check up on her. I walked into her bedroom, and saw that it had been trashed. Her belongings had been thrown everywhere.

The family dog was sitting at the end of the bed… Jenny was not there… I moved the curtain that separated her bedroom from her bathroom… And found her… Hanging from her shower rail with a broken neck.

I climbed onto the chair she had used to jump from and attempted to take her body weight off her neck, but I realized it was useless. I urgently called out to Nellie, our family housekeeper, to fetch and bring a pair of scissors, and as I cut my beautiful daughter down from the necktie noose she had made, I found myself mentally, physically and emotionally distraught on many levels.

Thinking rapidly... how to revive her... do I call someone for help... or run down the road to find a neighbor... do I stay and try to save her... Take action. Take action. Take action... Which first?

I dashed to the phone and called a friend and with frantic calm, ran down the road in order to find at-home neighbors. In the meantime, Nellie had run to call another neighbor from the other end of our street and on my returning to the house, this neighbor was exiting Jenny's room. She was deeply distressed, shocked, and in fright. She shouted at me, asking what had happened because my daughter was dead.

I knew then that there was nothing more I could do... it was over.

I collapsed in an anguished daze on the lawn outside the house, unable to move or take action anymore.

Part of me was desperate to bring Jenny back to life; the other part of me was filled with overwhelming relief that she was no longer able to hurt herself, that she was now 'safe' and no longer my responsibility. This had been her fourth attempt to kill herself and now she had finally succeeded.

I abstractly observed people come and people go. I watched the mortuary men arrive with their van, in order to prepare and take Jenny's body away. At one point (I have no recollection of doing it), when asked by the Police what had happened, I apparently beat my hands on the garage wall and cried out that I had killed Jenny and that it was my fault she was dead.

A little later, a crisis volunteer approached me and as she settled down on the grass to counsel me, her name badge read "Jenny". Even through my shock, my mind took note: "What a coincidence!"

The days that followed were combined with vivid accounts etched in my memory, together with happenings I inadvertently blanked out and had to be reminded about.

We held a church memorial service for Jen, which was followed by a 'celebration of her life' ceremony held in a marquee in our garden.

As I finally accepted that Jen was dead, I pondered the fact that she had been our most celebrated child — the much anticipated daughter after 2 boys. On her arrival, I felt blessed being able to experience that precious mom-daughter relationship.

Over the years and on the surface, Jenny appeared to be a mostly happy child with an engaging smile and an inquiring mind. From time to time, though, she displayed puzzling signs of irrationality and unreasonableness.

By way of example, when she was about 18 months old she created quite a stir in our neighborhood. I had collected her from kindergarten one lunch time, and whilst easing the car back into traffic, for no apparent reason, she began to cry. During the fifteen-minute journey back to our house, her cries built up to a bloodcurdling crescendo, as if she was being seriously attacked. Neighbors ran out of their houses to assist, and once we had removed her from the car, she just lay screaming, prostate on the pavement. For a good half an hour, absolutely nothing would console her and only once she had become completely spent did her screams finally end. Within 20 minutes, she was back to her normal self, interacting as though nothing had happened.

On another occasion when she was 4 years old, she accidentally spilt a flask of very hot water over herself. Her shrieks of pain transformed into anguished screaming, not because she was burning, but because she didn't want to expose her nipples to everyone present!

When she was 8, her best friend's family had invited her to join them for a celebratory birthday dinner at an upmarket restaurant. After I had taken her special party dress out of the cupboard for her to wear, Jen took a pair of scissors and cut a large hole in it so that she would have no choice but to go in her everyday clothes instead.

It came as a shock when shortly after she turned 13, Jenny claimed that she was the family outcast. She was convinced she had been swapped in the hospital as a baby because she felt she had never belonged to our family.

She also confessed to having secretly felt suicidal for most of her life, and that when she was about 7, she had tried whilst standing in front of her mirror, to choke herself to death with her hands. Friends and family were equally surprised with this revelation, as Jen mostly appeared to be a happy child.

As a teenager, after several suicide attempts and 2 sessions in rehab, she continued to battle with friends' verbal slights and their perceived insensitive actions, which had the capacity to shift her into a dark place emotionally. At this time her eating disorder kicked in, and overall her schoolwork took a nosedive, and it was very apparent that her self-worth and sense of purpose were severely compromised.

I once suggested to Jenny that she was taking life too seriously and that she should try to take her friends' actions more lightly and embrace these happenings as being a part of life and that she had the ability to choose to feel differently.

Her answer was "... but Mum, everyone is presuming that I feel like everyone else. This is the way I feel, and it is very real to me. How and what everyone else feels and how they cope does not help me."

At 13, Jen was expelled from rehab hospital for "bad behavior" after attempting to overdose and cut her wrists in the gardens outside her ward. She and 2 other adolescent patients subsequently ran away into the streets of Johannesburg. We lost her for 30 hours straight, and I feared that we would never see or hear of her again. She was eventually found locked in a house not too far away from the place they had run away from. Those 30 very long hours felt equal to the missing years of Jesus up until he was 30 years old. No one really knows what happened and what Christ had to work through in those unknown years before he emerged as an insightful adult, and I suppose much the same applies to Jen. Nobody really knows what was happening deep inside her in what appeared to be her "missing" times.

Sitting in my bedroom in the UK two years later, and I'm planning a way to effectively end my life. I found a route by train and chose a self-catering flat to book in a town far away from anyone who would know me. It was there that I intended to gas myself in the oven.

Thank God I... ® *Am an Empowered Woman:*

On the eve of my departure whilst packing my bags, I unexpectedly received a phone call from my brother. We had previously agreed that I would text him my arrival time once I had boarded the train to Oxford the following day, but for some reason he chose to call me the night before to ask for my arrival time. It was this phone call that "kicked" me out of my initial focus and which enabled me to process that with my cancer, these challenging circumstances could change. I re-planned my train route and arrived safely at my brother's flat.

In hindsight, I can now understand the difference between Jen's and my emotional pain. In parenting Jenny, I so often observed how no particular set of parenting skills consistently worked for or with her. Sometimes dealing with her issues worked by applying one approach and yet the next time, the same approach created the opposite reaction and outcome from her. Her inconsistency in being able to process and live within important parameters made it more than challenging to interact with her as a parent. Now I can more easily understand that the circumstances that motivated Jen to take her life were existential and that the circumstances that led to my wanting to end my life were circumstantial.

In experiencing the emotional pain of almost leaving this world, I was finally able to understand the reasonableness of Jen killing herself. Even though her suicide was unreasonable by my and society's standards, I now equally understand the unreasonableness in living a long life and that Jenny's uniqueness in deciding to leave the planet was a reasonable decision for her. She had her own reasons which made her able-to-reason — "reason-able".

Post-Jenny, I spent much time working on myself through meditating, facilitating intuitive workshops, and at the same time, spending time equilibrating my deep grief and loss. Through working a 14 column-equilibrating chart I was able to shift the story in my head about my memory of Jenny, and open up to a deeper understanding of that memory. This balancing process enabled me to shift the story I had in my head that my life was dreadful, and I was able to experience a complete understanding that as much as Jenny's death has been a deep loss, it has also created just as much deep meaning and a sense of purpose.

With new clarity, I see that Jen danced to the beat of her own drum and that leaving the planet was about transforming into something else. I have experienced her in many 'new' ways. That 'coincidental' happening with social worker Jenny on my lawn was an initial sign of this. Many more indications made me aware that losing her was part of the cycle of change and that we had not really lost her, but that her energy had changed form. It was these revelations that formed the creation of my book, *Full-Circle Rainbow*.

I have watched how my children have worked through the loss of their sister and have become inspired mostly because of what happened. By way of example, my youngest daughter, after having successfully completed high school, has dedicated herself to studying psychology at University, thus embracing the very vision and focus that her sister had battled so hard to apply.

Jen's self-worth and lack of purpose has and is helping people to find the self-worth and purpose that she never felt. Self-worth, purpose, and being "reasonable" are recurring themes within my Grief Coaching work, and I realize that Jenny has been with me all along, assisting other people — through me and as an extension of me — with the use of self-worth and purpose. She is with them and with me and that's the transformation.

Thank God I... *Am an Empowered Woman:*

♥♥♥

Jenetta Barry is a Grief Specialist, Life Coach, and Author. After the death of her daughter, Jenetta dedicated her life to healing her loss. By combining her experience and teachings, Jenetta has assisted many to heal and gain a different and deeper understanding and appreciation of their life challenges. Jenetta presents talks and seminars and conducts consultations both on Skype and face-to-face. She is Mum to Stuart, Neil, Jenny, and Catherine, as well as a Gran to 4 year-old twins, Malaika and Alexa. Visit her at <u>JenettaBarry.com</u>

Thank God I...
By Sheila Gale

I was alone and doubled over on my knees in the courtyard, sobbing and begging God to take this pain away. I prayed that a year would hurry up and pass, so this gut-wrenching physical and mental anguish would subside. My kids were my world, and now they were spending half of the time, half of their lives, living with their father and his new wife, who can't stand me! Earlier that day, he came to pick them up. Natasha, only 5, had to be shoved into the car, her little arms reaching out for me, wailing "Mommy, Mommy. No, no, Mommy!" I wanted to die. That wasn't an option, because of the children, but it seemed like a far better answer than this nightmare called my life.

The metals jewelry class at the college was helpful, kind of like therapy; along with a real therapist, and of course, medicating myself with pills as a temporary fix. But worse than my pain, was the pain that my decision caused to my two precious children. It was almost unbearable.

Shelly was in my class, and she thought I was funny and loved hearing my stories about my years in Hollywood, as a bit actor and a music radio personality. One day she came to class with a phone number and name of a local talk radio station looking for people to have a show. "You should try this, Sheila."

"Nope, been there, done that." I knew it was some small station that you had to pay for the hour, and while having my own talk show was always a dream of mine, I wasn't interested. She wouldn't let up. I took the number and went home.

Thank God I... ® *Am an Empowered Woman:*

A week later I awoke to a day filled with sunshine. Blue jays and crows were squawking. I always fed them unsalted peanuts in the shell. I stayed in bed late this morning, not wanting to get up. The kids were still with their dad. I thought about going to buy silver from the coin shop to make another cuff bracelet in my jewelry class. As I started to drive away, I suddenly stopped at the end of the driveway. I looked at the piece of paper with the name and address of the station on my car seat.

I said, "Okay, God, what do you want me to do? Do I go buy silver, or do I try to find this radio station?" I sat there for about two minutes, and instead of turning left towards the coin shop, my car turned right and I was on my way to somewhere in Sand City about 4 miles away.

Questioning myself during the drive, I finally found this place tucked away in an industrial part of the city. I realized I had coffee stains on my leggings, no make-up, not very professional looking at all. I walked into the office and asked to speak to the station manager.

"What's your name?" the receptionist asked.

"Sheila Gale," I answered.

She told me the manager would be out in a few minutes. Ten minutes later, Hal, the station owner, walked in, shook my hand, and led me to the production room. "How can I help you?" he asked as he was totally looking at his computer and typing away. Awfully rude, I thought! "I want my own radio show." He kept staring at his computer.

"What would it be about?"

"Uhhh... day-to-day stuff. Yeah! Day-to-Day with Sheila Gale," I made it up on the spot.

"How much can you spend? Can you work Saturdays at 4pm?"

"Yes."

I then looked at his computer screen and realized he had been Googling me and was reading all about me, my past as a radio host in L.A, and movie stuff. Wow! I didn't even know I was documented. That really helped seal the deal.

"Can you start next week?" "Sure." I had no idea what I was going to do or what I would talk about. He walked me into the live studio, and when I saw that microphone and the mixing board, a surge of excitement filled my entire being for the first time in 20 years.

On my first show I had Charlie, my gay friend, and Katie, a sex addict, talking about their sexual exploits. It went okay, and I had no expectations of what or where this show would go, or not go. I just knew this was something that was positive in my life right now. With the horrors of divorce and my constant quest for a better life, this was something good.

The moment that red light went on, and I heard my voice talking over the music in my headphones for the first time in 15 years, an indescribable feeling of power, calm, and elation filled me. I wasn't depressed when I was on the air. Weeks turned into months, and months turned into that year I had prayed about.

But I still was not much better. I hated my life! I was numbing myself with anxiety and pain pills, while constantly praying for answers. I was driving to Whole Foods, and I started to scream at God in the car. I didn't care who saw or heard me!

"You think this is some kind of sick game?! Ha ha, let's have you all suffer and struggle in this life, and see if you can find me?! Ha, what a sick little game. God, you need to give me a sign of hope *right now*!"

With that, I turned on the car radio, and it was a talk station. I heard some woman saying, "Yes, our manifestation seminar will be in Carmel next week, and we have Michael Beckwith from 'The Secret' as our special guest." Followed by, "Great to have you on, we're out of time, goodbye".

Wait, what?! Who was that? I immediately called that station and asked what show that was and who the guest was. Her name was Mari Cooper, a psychic and powerful teacher of manifesting abundance. I got her number and asked her to be on my upcoming show. She agreed (I immediately canceled my other guest). I read all I could about her on her website, and two days later, we were laughing and talking all about her upcoming seminar. At the end of the show she said, "Sheila, I'd like to gift you this 3 day class." What? and spend an evening with Michael Beckwith? Hell yes! The class was $1,600. Thank you God, and continue.

I asked God for clarity on what I was to do every day. I noticed that my dependency on prescription drugs was not working anymore, but the thought of being totally sober in life scared the shit out of me! Another thing that started happening was that publicists and bestselling authors were contacting *me* to interview their clients and authors. Some of these people had been on Oprah!

I also realized that I was moving toward all self-help, human potential leaders, and visionaries as my guests. And I slowly started to get better. My progress was at a snail's pace, but some of these people were amazing and they had what I wanted! A life that worked and flourished. They had answers.

I took whatever resonated with me and left the rest. I took baby steps. Through much desire and knowing that life should and could be extraordinary (without knowing how), I persevered. With my doctor's help and lots of walks in The Redwoods, I was able to get off all medication. (Really hard!) Still there was this constant gnawing inside me, a yearning, knowing something bigger was waiting for me, yet I had not a clue what it was.

That feeling had been there my whole life. I squelched it with alcohol in my twenties, with bad relationships in my thirties, and now at fifty, I was starting over. This radio show was now going on 3 years, still paying a few hundred dollars a month with maybe 2 or 3 sponsors (basically barely covering the costs).

Alimony was running out, and my child support was being reduced. "How am I ever going to make a real living, God?!" I have never made more than $15 an hour, no college education, and I'm 50.

I was outside watering and looking at all the dead flowers and trees I had planted back in better days. Not able to afford a gardener, I really looked at how hard my life was, and I said, "God I need help!" In the next second, two young men walked around the corner and startled me. I sized them up — ties, white shirts, badges, and a Bible. Okay, here we go, a couple of holy rollers!

Thank God I... ® *Am an Empowered Woman:*

"Excuse me, Ma'am, we're Mormons, and we'd like to share about Jesus Christ." To which I replied, "Thank you, but I have God, and we talk every day."

He looked around at the yard and continued, "No offense, Ma'am, but it really looks like you can use some help here. We'd like to help you, we're Missionaries."

I asked God for help one minute ago! I burst into tears and told them, "No, no, that's okay." "Please, please let us help you. This is what we do." They had no idea why I was sobbing.

The next day, they came back in jeans and tee shirts (and badges) and filled up my green can. The next week, they came back with four more Missionaries and filled up my green can and my neighbors' can. The following week they came back with 10 others and took a huge load to the dump! They have been a part of my life for nearly three years now. Not only did I have them on my radio show, I took them to The Redwoods, made them dinner, and even went to church once. I love Mormons!! They are some of the nicest people I have ever met. Thank you God and continue.

Shortly after, I had an interior designer on my show and she said she'd like to give me a free consultation (a $200 value). When she arrived, I told her I really couldn't afford to buy anything, but that my friend wanted to give me a really big desk and I had the measurements. So she walked around the house measuring spaces and said, "If you put the desk in this room and move the TV in here, it will work."

A week later, this giant 3 piece desk arrived, and my precious Mormon friends put it all together in what used to be the family room. I remember thinking, "What in the hell am I going to do with this giant desk?!" I literally had

$2,000 in my account, my income was being cut in half, and my mortgage payment was going up $1,000 in 2 months.

"God, you need to show me what to do!" I had applied for a home modification program, to reduce the payment, but got rejected twice. I got the hunch to call again. You never know who you'll talk to, always someone different. This time I got a tough black woman who read over my applications and said, "You're going to get rejected again with these numbers, and you can't apply anymore."

I started to cry and then I asked, "What would it take for me to get approved?" For the next twenty minutes she had me go over every line, asking: "How much is your grocery bill a week?" I'd say $300. She'd say, "Well if you said $100 that would be better." "$100!" I exclaimed. "How much do you pay for utilities?" "$350" I answered. "Well, if you said $150 that would be better." "$150!" I replied. "Now, if you fill out that form just like I said, I'll get you a negotiator."

"OMG! Thank you so much! What's your name?"

"Faith." I began sobbing, "Faith!! I am going to tell everyone about you Faith on my radio show. Thank you God and continue.

Four days later a FedEx man arrived with an envelope. I couldn't imagine what I had ordered. When I opened the envelope, it stated, "You have been approved for a home modification. Your monthly payment for the next year is $486.00, then $750.00 for three years, then $1,200.00 for the 5th year." Did I mention this doesn't affect my credit? Holy shit! I had just called a realtor to see about selling my house. My payment would have gone up to $3,000. Thank you God and continue!

Thank God I... ® *Am an Empowered Woman:*

I had been pounding the pavement trying to monetize my interviews. The guests were people like Byron Katie, Gregg Braden, Marci Shimoff from 'The Secret,' and even a six-time Oprah guest. I had contacted every syndicated radio station and nobody was going to discover me.

I was sitting in the courtyard watching the blue jays when the phone rang. "Hello, Sheila, this is Brad Codd, and I produce teleseminars. Are you ready to make lots and lots of money?"

I knew immediately who he was and the tremendous success other hosts had had working with him. I saw everything in a flash, stumbling into the radio station, the Mormons arriving, the modification, the huge desk arriving, and this moment was why it all happened in perfect Divine timing. I was being prepared for my higher calling.

I never saw it at the time, but that's how it all works. The Universe has our back.

Within the next 12 months, I put a roof on our house, took my kids to Hawaii to swim with the dolphins, and made more money than I have ever made or ever thought possible. I do what I love and am passionate about, and I get to help people every day. There is a way, a formula for living this life. It is through our darkest hours that we get guidance if we ask. I finally get to live the life I knew was possible, yet had no idea why it wasn't happening.

What if life is just as easy as, "Ask and receive?" What if we started asking more questions, like what else is possible? Or what are the infinite possibilities for my life? What if life's answers are actually in the question? How does it get any better than this?!

Awakening Your Inner Strength and Genius...

♥♥♥

Sheila Gale is one of the world's top syndicated radio hosts in the Inspirational, Spiritual, Energy Healing, and Human Potential movement.

Sheila's quick wit and willingness to openly share her candid struggles with depression and addiction on her daily LIVE radio show, *The Sheila Show: Inspiration For Your Life*, give listeners a presence of "realness" that is sadly lacking on today's airwaves. Her courageous and genuine on-air style and Sheila's enthusiasm for life makes her a Master Motivator. A true healer, and Deeksha Blessing Giver, Sheila is also an Access Consciousness Facilitator, leading workshops worldwide.

Sheila is also a top Teleseminar Leader and hosts a-list speakers like Joe Vitale, Marci Shimoff and John Assaraff from *The Secret*. Also Doreen Virtue, Byron Katie, Sonia Choquette, Gregg Braden, Dr. Norm Shealy and hundreds more.

Thank God I am a Resilient Woman
By Prof. Susana Ethel de Pereda

I was born in Montevideo, Uruguay, my family home. When Leonardo, my son, was a toddler of 3 years old, we thought it would be a great opportunity to expand our horizons by living abroad for at least two years.

Initially, I wanted to live in Canada, because I had friends living in Vancouver, but when we went to apply for a Visa, there were none available.

So we thought, which other country was looking for extra people? Well, Australia was looking for people with suitable qualifications, and although extremely far away from where I was born, we decided to take our chances and explore what Australia could offer. We thought this could be a great adventure.

We were granted Visa's as permanent residents, and we were jumping with joy. As we approached the great adventure of our lives, we shared our happiness with our family members; not realizing what a tremendous emotional impact it would have on them.

They were all so happy for us... not showing their true feelings. I promised my dad that I would be back in 2 years. I was unaware, being totally occupied with the excitement of travelling from Uruguay to Australia; that the move would cause me and my immediate family such enormous emotional upheaval.

I personally wanted to return home immediately, and my son wanted to go back with my mum, his grandmother, but we could not do that. We had signed a contract to remain in Australia for 2 years.

Leonardo lost a lot of weight, poor darling. He did not like the Australian food and could not yet understand English. He followed me everywhere saying, "Please, mamita, take me back with grandma." It was really heartbreaking, and the only thing I could do was to reassure him that, "We will see them soon." As my son kept losing weight, I was putting it on.

I would cry myself to sleep at night, but I didn't allow that to stop me from trying to find work and getting on with my life. I was in Australia for a reason, and I was going to follow it through.

I had a Plan that I wanted to execute, and with my skills in teaching, journalism, and marketing, I began to put it all together. This Plan was going to help other people in the same situation as myself and also the multicultural Australian society at large.

The Plan was presented to the Government Department that I was working with at the time, and it was accepted. Dozens of programs were set up for various areas such as Education, Training, Arts and Crafts, Children's education of all ages, Recreation, Radio, and TV, et cetera. The Plan was put into place and in many ways expanded and became very successful.

Some years later in the course of following up with groups and organizations which had been granted funds for cultural, sports, and social activities, I spoke to those groups that had received the grants. I became suspicious and alerted to the fact that the system had been seriously abused. Although the grants were approved and allocated, they were apparently not received. I also sensed a personal danger because of the discoveries that I had made.

Once again, I experienced an emotional upheaval because my Plan had been manipulated and compromised. I felt cheated, angry, let down, and bitterly disappointed. I felt sick in the stomach.

On the day of my discovery, I took the train the same time as I usually did to go home. The trip was over an hour, and I used this time to design and create a plan of action for myself and my work.

That night after dinner, I worked late until my plan was ready. A plan to be executed when I thought the time was right. The following days at work, I attended to my duties as usual, remaining professional and helpful with a happy and smiling attitude towards everyone, as my normal self.

Weeks went by, and I decided to take some time off. On the first day of my holiday, I received a letter from my mum letting me know that my dad had his third heart attack. This was the tip of the iceberg for me, I cried so loud that a neighbor across the road came and helped me through my despair. I called my mum, who told me not to return home to see my dad, as he was getting better.

Christmas was almost upon us, and I kept in touch with mum, until the 23rd of December, my and she kept saying that dad was stable. Through Christmas and the first days of the New Year, I kept calling my mum, but her phone was always busy.

During the Christmas period, I moved to my new apartment, and in the process, all mail went to the previous address. It was early January when my husband collected the post and came back with a bundle of letters. He said that there was a letter from my mum which he wanted to read to me.

I felt sick in the stomach as if I knew what had happened... My dad had passed away on Christmas day, his favorite day of the year. I felt so sick, empty, hopeless, filled with sadness and grief. I felt so much guilt and frustration, my mum and my family were so far away.

Initially, I was very angry with my mum that she had denied me the time to be with my dad, by preventing me from visiting my dad when he was ill. My next emotion was to cry uncontrollably for quite some time. When I calmed down, I knew that it was time to execute "The Plan" that I created 2 months ago.

Two months earlier, I had found out that some people had taken personal advantage of my Plan and projects for their own financial gain, contrary to everything I had worked for. When my holiday was finished, I went back to work. Lunch time came along quicker than I expected, and I decided to take a long walk and arrived at Sydney Harbor. Every detail around me was refreshing, the beautiful scenery with boats and yachts. I enjoyed the scenery and fresh air, couples having lunch in the cafes al fresco, the children playing in the nearby park, the noise of all the birds. I had lunch, and on my return to the office, I gave my resignation in writing, effective in one month, as per contract.

Following my decision I felt FREE AS A BIRD, although I knew that some hiccups would arise as my husband had been out of work for some time, and I was the bread winner. My decision to resign was carefully calculated by me two months earlier.

Thank God I... ® *Am an Empowered Woman:*

My apartment was paid in full, and I had applied for other positions. After resigning, major changes were taking place, a new life was being born. I could not agree with the system, and by resigning, I felt like a weight was being lifted. I thought, there is no need to be concerned, everything will work out in the end.

Suddenly I felt the same emotions that I had felt when I arrived in Australia. Which made me even consider going back home to be with family; however, I immediately realized that I was grieving, and I prayed. I prayed for God to give me an abundance of Love to keep me going ahead with Hope.

I was very proud of myself, knowing that I had contributed in many ways to Australia, making a difference for everyone, regardless of gender, nationality or religion.

This new lesson, once more, made me realize... Thank God I Am A Resilient Woman.

I was born in Montevideo, Uruguay and I arrived to Sydney, Australia, in 1971 with my husband and my 3 ½-year-old son, Leonardo. In 1982, I moved to Perth, Western Australia. Now, I am divorced and Leonardo has three children, two sons and one daughter — Theo 5 years old, Felix 3 years, and Veronica 2 years — who are my pride and joy.

Susana is the Founder and CEO of the LIFE GUIDE INTERNATIONAL trade mark, running courses *How to Become a Life Guide* combined with her other Teachings.

www.ingramcontent.com/pod-product-compliance
Lightning Source LLC
Chambersburg PA
CBHW061255110426
42742CB00012BA/1927